Build a Better Mousetrap

Build a Better Mousetrap

Make Classic Inventions, Discover Your Problem-Solving Genius, and Take the Inventor's Challenge

RUTH KASSINGER

John Wiley & Sons, Inc.

ISBN 0-471-39538-2

Printed in the United States of America

10 9 8 7 6 5 4 3 2 1

For my sister, Joan Good,
who is so generous in her enthusiasm

Contents

Acknowledgments

Thanks are due, once again, to Dr. Burton Edelson and James Polk as consultants in science and engineering, as well as to Dr. Charles Bahn, the people at Peterson Electro-Musical Products and The Kazoo Company, and my editor, Kate Bradford. As always, I am grateful for the wholehearted support of my husband, Ted, and daughters, Anna, Austen, and Alice.

Build a Better Mousetrap

Introduction

"Build a better mousetrap," the American philosopher Ralph Waldo Emerson said in 1855, "and the world will beat a path to your door." When Emerson spoke of mousetraps, he didn't mean just mousetraps. He meant any kind of invention that solves a problem. Emerson could have said, "Build a stronger bridge," "Build a more accurate clock," or "Build a better device for listening to the heart."

When Emerson said, "and the world will beat a path to your door," he meant that when people see a better design, they will hustle over to the inventor to buy it (trampling a path in the grass on the way). As you'll see in this book, when an Italian invented spectacles in the thirteenth century, people no longer used the chunky "reading stones" to help them see. After French doctor René Laënnec invented the stethoscope in 1816, every doctor had to have one. And when Simon Lake invented the periscope in 1902, his submarine was suddenly in demand by the U.S. Navy. We are always on the lookout for devices that make our lives better, easier, or more fun, and we're usually quick to drop the old for the new.

> **Many Americans have taken Emerson literally in the last 150 years: The U.S. Patent Office has issued over 4,400 patents for original mousetraps. (Thousands more applications have been rejected as unoriginal.) Mousetraps have been the most frequently invented device in U.S. history, although the old, familiar spring trap is still the most popular.**

So, how do you go about making an invention that will bring the world to your door? The first step is to identify a problem. Sometimes the problem is obvious. When the young French balloonist Andre-Jacques Garnerin was imprisoned in a Hungarian castle in 1793, he quickly identified his problem: he needed a way to escape. He dreamed up the parachute as a result.

The next step in inventing is observing the world around you. In ancient Egypt, someone invented the water clock after noticing that water dripped at a steady rate from containers with a hole in the bottom. In 1891, American Clarence Kemp observed that metal painted black retains heat well, and he used his observation to invent the solar water heater.

After identifying a problem and making observations, it's time to experiment . . . and experiment . . . and experiment. None of the inventions in this book worked out perfectly the first time. Christopher Cockerell,

I n 1760, Joseph Merlin, a London instrument maker, invented the first roller skates. (He introduced his invention to the world by skating into a party wearing boots with large wheels strapped to them and playing the violin. The wheels worked well, but the brakes didn't. He crashed into a huge glass mirror, which shattered around him.) Inventors tinkered with and refined roller skates for 220 years, making them smaller, better, and easier to wear. Then, in 1979, Scott and Brennan Olson, hockey-playing brothers from Minnesota, made a major improvement to roller skates. They arranged the wheels in a row, rather than at four corners like the wheels on a car, and invented in-line skates.

Roller skates are still evolving, thanks to inventors who keep experimenting. Now you can buy shoes with rollers on the bottom that retract into the bottom of the shoes so that you can go from walking to rolling in a flash. Who knows where the roller skate will go next?

inventor of the hovercraft, took years to make a working boat. Even after the first one was built, he continued to improve it. Domemico Salsano invented a seismograph (a device that measures the intensity of earthquakes) in 1783, but it took generations of inventors to perfect Salsano's device. Alan Adler spent 10 years, from 1975 to 1985, making changes to the Frisbee before he perfected the best-selling toy, the Aerobie.

Each of the first 21 chapters in this book helps you reinvent an invention. In each chapter, you'll learn about a problem an inventor faced and what he or she observed that helped solve the problem. Then, you'll find a list of materials and directions so that you can reinvent the invention, either full-size or as a model. Next, you'll learn about the history of the invention and find out how the original inventor solved the problem. At the end of each chapter, you'll find an inventor's challenge so that you can apply your inventing skills to a related problem. Finally, when you get to the last chapter, you will face the ultimate inventor's challenge: Can you build a better mousetrap?

PART I

Inventions That Use Light

We have been experimenting with light since our prehistoric ancestors first lit fires. Our ancestors didn't know it, but now we know that light is a form of energy. Light is packets of energy called **photons.** When the packets are traveling through a **vacuum**—a space that is empty of all matter—they travel very fast (186,000 miles or 300,000 km per second) in a straight line.

When light encounters matter, such as the gases in the Earth's atmosphere, water, or a mirror, it no longer travels in a straight line. The path of the photons is changed. Some kinds of matter, such as mirrors, **reflect** (bounce back) the light. Others, such as water, **refract** (bend) the light so that it passes through at an

angle. If photons hit a pane of clear glass at a *right angle* (a 90°
angle), they pass through without change.

The ancient Mesopotamians experimented with reflected light
and, as early as 1500 B.C., invented mirrors made of shiny metals.
The ancient Greeks figured out how to focus reflected light off a
curved mirror to start a fire. (Archimedes is said to have set enemy
ships on fire with a huge version of such a mirror, but that's probably a tall tale.) As you will see in this section, inventors in the
nineteenth and twentieth centuries used reflected light to make
the kaleidoscope and the periscope.

People have long noticed that light is refracted when it passes
through water. (Next time you're at a pool, stand in the water and
stretch out your arm under water. It will look as though your arm
is broken because the light reflecting off your arm is slowed down
and bent by the water.) Once glassmakers learned to make transparent glass, inventors noticed that light was also bent by glass.
They put their observations to use and created a multitude of
devices including magnifying glasses, spectacles, telescopes, and
microscopes, which worked by bending light. Gem cutters around
the world learned how to shape *transparent* (clear) and *translucent*
(almost clear) minerals so that light refracted within them and
reflected off them, making them sparkle.

Until about A.D. 1000, most people thought that eyes produced
or *emitted* light, which then bounced off objects so that they were
seen. Then, Arab mathematician Al-hazen suggested that eyes
receive light that comes to them. Slowly, over the following centuries, scientists came to understand the workings of the eye and
how the brain interprets the light it receives. The phenakistiscope,
which you will find described in this section, resulted from an
optical scientist's study of how long the brain sees images.

1 Spectacles

The Problem

You are a glassmaker on the island city of Venice (in what is today Italy) in the late 1200s. You and your fellow craftspeople at the Venetian glass factories are renowned throughout Europe for the beautiful, light, transparent blown-glass objects you make. You love your work and are expert in decorating glass with intricate patterns of gold, silver, and enamel threads melted on its surface.

You are now 45 years old and, unfortunately, your eyesight is declining. In order to clearly see the object you are working on, you need to hold it almost at arm's length. Soon, your arms won't be long enough! You don't want to give up your craft. What can you do?

Glass is made from sand, sodium carbonate (a chemical found in the ashes of burned vegetation or as deposits in the earth), and lime, which is chalk. The ingredients must be combined at temperatures of about 2,500° F (1,400°C). No one knows for certain who invented glass, but glass dating to 2250 B.C. was found in Mesopotamia, the area between the Tigris and Euphrates Rivers (in what is now Iraq). It may be that Mesopotamian potters created glass by accident. They needed to bake their pots at high temperatures to make them hard and waterproof. In heating the pots, they may have fused sand and some minerals on the surface of the pot, making a glassy surface.

At first, people made only beads out of glass. Then, they discovered they could pour hot glass into molds and form cups and other useful objects. About 1000 B.C., glassmakers learned how to blow glass into shapes. By blowing through a long metal pipe into a blob of molten (melted) glass, they could create bubbles in the glass. The bubbles could then be shaped into glasses and bowls and even flat pieces.

Observations

Because the glass made at your factory is quite clear, it is especially good for making "reading stones." A reading stone—an invention that the Europeans borrowed from the Arabs—is a hemisphere of clear glass that a reader places, flat-side down, on a page. The letters directly beneath the center of the stone are greatly enlarged, making it possible for people with failing eyesight to read.

A reading stone is cumbersome and only works when lying flat on a page, so it wouldn't help you at all. But, it gives you an idea . . .

MATERIALS

small pot

water

spoon

package of unflavored gelatin

small bowl as nearly hemispherical (half of a globe) as possible

page from a newspaper or magazine

plastic wrap

pan

two small plastic resealable bags about 1¼ × 1¼ inches (3 × 3 cm), available at craft stores

tape

Experiments

1. Use the small pot, water, and spoon to prepare one package of gelatin according to the package instructions.

2. Fill the bowl with gelatin. Put the bowl in the refrigerator.

3. Cover a page from a newspaper or magazine with a piece of plastic wrap.

4. When the gelatin is completely solid, remove the bowl from the refrigerator. Put the bowl in a pan of hot water so that the water level is just below the rim of the bowl. Wait 1 minute. Turn the bowl upside-down on top of the newspaper. A dome-shaped block of gelatin should slip out. (If it doesn't, put the bowl back in the hot water for another minute.) This is your reading stone.

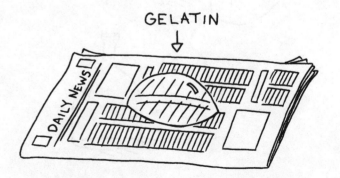

GELATIN

5. Observe how the reading stone magnifies the words beneath it. Lift your reading stone from the page and look through it. Does it still work?

6. Fill one of the resealable bags with water and seal it. Note how the bag looks when you view it from the side. Try placing the bag directly on the page. Does it make the print look larger? Hold the bag flat a few inches above the page and look down through it. Does this make the print look larger? Experiment with holding the bag close to your eye, and then, with your other hand, moving the page toward your eye. At what distance does the print look the largest?

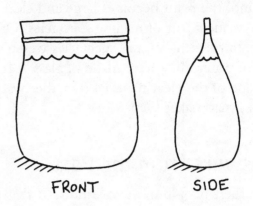

RESEALABLE BAGS WITH WATER

FRONT   SIDE

7. Fill the other resealable bag with water and seal it. Take the plastic wrap off the newspaper or magazine page and tape the page to a wall

A magnifying (enlarging) lens has two surfaces. One of the surfaces must have an outwardly curving (**convex**) shape. The other surface can be flat or also convex. When a magnifying lens has two convex surfaces (meaning the lens is **biconvex**), each surface magnifies. A biconvex lens is slimmer and weighs less than a lens with only one convex surface.

Convex lenses bend light in a way that makes objects appear larger. When you hold a magnifying lens in front of your eye, the light reflecting from the page toward your eye bends. Your brain assumes, however, that the light rays have reached your eyes in the usual way, in a straight line. Your brain traces the path of the light back in a straight line, to where it would have come from if it hadn't been refracted by the lens. You actually see a "virtual" image of the page. The enlarged virtual image isn't real: your brain has constructed it!

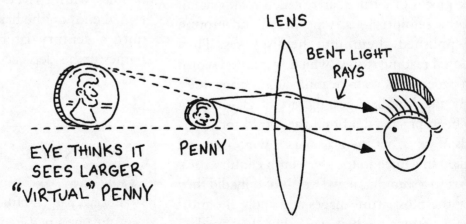

LENS

BENT LIGHT RAYS

EYE THINKS IT SEES LARGER "VIRTUAL" PENNY

PENNY

or other surface at eye level. Hold a water-filled bag in front of each eye and approach the page until the print becomes large and clear. You've made a pair of reading spectacles! Of course, thirteenth-century spectacles weren't made of water; they were made of glass. It is the shape of the clear material (whether water or glass) that makes them work.

Answers from the Past

The earliest people must have noticed that the domed shape of a water drop on a flat surface makes whatever lies beneath it look larger. Ancient Greek and Roman writers remarked on the fact that a glass globe filled with water would magnify items placed in it or behind it. It wasn't until the Middle Ages, sometime after A.D. 1100, that people put the magnifying ability of a clear, curved surface to work.

When the Crusaders returned from their efforts to recapture Jerusalem in the 1100s, they brought back the writings of a gifted Arab mathematician named Al-hazen. Among Al-hazen's works were detailed studies of precisely how light is refracted by water and glass and how images are magnified. European monks read Al-hazen with interest. As avid readers (and among the few literate people of the time), they recognized the practical value of his studies. They took pieces of clear quartz (called rock crystal) and the semiprecious stone beryl, and ground and polished them into hemispheres. They invented reading stones, which magnified words on a page just as your gelatin reading stone does.

By the Middle Ages, the art of glassmaking had been practiced around the world for thousands of years, but the glassmakers who lived and worked in Venice in the thirteenth century took the art to a stunning new level. Not only did they blow the most artful shapes and apply the most elegant designs to their work, but they worked with very clear glass. Rock crystal and beryl were expensive, so the glassmakers found a ready market for reading stones made out of glass.

No one knows exactly who invented spectacles, but we do know they were invented in Italy in the last few decades of the thirteenth century. An aging Venetian glass craftsman could have been the inventor. This person would have had the skills to make lenses. He also would have had the motivation to make them: most people over the age of 40 develop **presbyopia,** which means an inability to see close objects clearly.

> **P**resbyopia has Greek roots. *Presby* means "old man" in Greek and *opia* means "relating to the eyes." If you have presbyopia, you have "old man eyes."

Whoever invented spectacles would have made a fortune if there had been patent laws in the thirteenth century. Spectacles to remedy presbyopia caught on immediately, and their use spread quickly across Europe. At first, people simply held the lenses, one in each hand, and looked through them. A little later, they encircled each lens with a metal or wooden frame and a bit of a handle and attached the ends of the handles with a rivet. The wearer balanced the joined ends on the bridge of his nose! It was not until a century later that someone invented frames with sidepieces that wrapped around the ears.

INVENTOR'S CHALLENGE

Using the two lenses you made and other materials you can find around the house, can you invent a new device (not the traditional frame for glasses) that will hold the lenses in place in front of, but not touching, your eyes?

2 Kaleidoscope

The Problem

It is 1814, and you are a Scottish scientist interested in optics (the study of light and vision). One day, as you are handling two pieces of glass and experimenting with how light passes from one surface to another, you notice something interesting: When you position the two pieces of glass in a shallow V shape, you see that an image of a candle across the room is reflected many times in a circular pattern.

Several months later, when working with two pieces of gold and silver, you notice the phenomenon again. The pattern of the images reflected off the V of polished metals is strikingly beautiful. You wonder what causes these repetitive reflections: What are the mathematics behind this phenomenon? You also delight in the beauty and the elegant symmetry of what you see, and wonder if you can make a device that consistently creates these types of images.

Observations

Telescopes, with their various arrangements of mirrors and lenses in a tube, have always intrigued you. You built your first one when you were 10 years old. Would a telescope be a good model to use for a new optical instrument?

MATERIALS

two identical, tubular potato chip canisters (with plastic end caps) approximately 9 inches (23 cm) tall and 3 inches (7.5 cm) in diameter. One canister must be empty. Only a plastic end cap is needed from the second canister.

can opener

paper towels

dime

pencil

scissors

ruler

sheet of clear, semirigid plastic that can be cut with scissors. You'll need at least a 6- × 6-inch (15- × 15-cm) piece. Acetate (available in sheets from a craft shop) works well, or plastic from vacuum-packaged pasta and other products.

glue

9- × 7-inch (23- × 18-cm) piece of stiff, non-corrugated cardboard (shoebox cardboard works well)

10- × 8-inch (25- × 21-cm) piece of silvery Mylar (you can use a Mylar balloon or Mylar wrapping paper)

sheet of black construction paper

transparent tape

small, colorful objects such as beads, trinkets, colored paper clips, or buttons

Experiment

1. Take the end caps off the potato chip canisters and set them aside.

2. Use the can opener to remove the metal end from the empty potato chip canister.

Discard the metal end. Clean the inside of the canister with a paper towel. (Caution: Watch out for the cut metal ends both on the piece you discard and inside the canister!)

3. Center the dime on one of the plastic end caps, use a pencil to trace a circle around it, and cut out the circle. Discard the circle.

4. Cut a 2- × 2-inch (5- × 5-cm) square from the clear, semirigid plastic and glue it over the hole on the inside of the end cap. Save the rest of the plastic for Step 11. Put the cap (which is now the eyepiece for your kaleidoscope) back on the canister.

5. Spread a thin coat of glue on the cardboard. Press and smooth the Mylar onto the cardboard. Trim the Mylar to fit the cardboard.

6. Using the ruler, make two lines on the Mylar-covered cardboard so that the cardboard is divided into three 8- × 2-inch (20- × 5-cm) rectangles. Cut the cardboard carefully along the lines. Now you have three mirrors.

7. Cut an 8- × 2-inch (20- × 5-cm) piece of black construction paper and tape it over one mirror. Use only a little tape at each end so that the cover will be easy to remove later.

8. Lay the three mirrors next to each other, face down, with about 1/16 inch (1 mm) between each mirror. Place three pieces of tape across the backs of the mirrors, as shown.

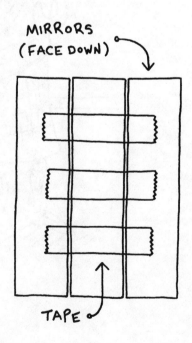

MIRRORS (FACE DOWN)

TAPE

9. Bend the three mirrors into a triangular shape with the mirrors inside, as shown. Tape the last seam closed. Look through the end of the mirrors and see what the world looks like.

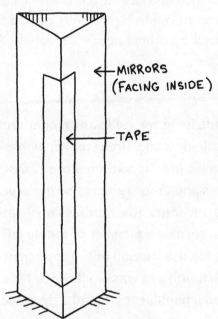

MIRRORS
(FACING INSIDE)

TAPE

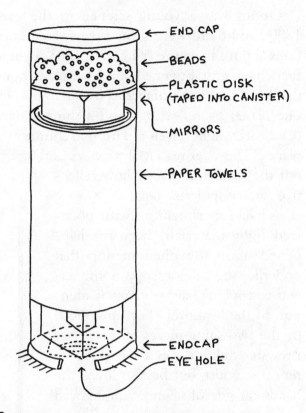

END CAP

BEADS

PLASTIC DISK
(TAPED INTO CANISTER)

MIRRORS

PAPER TOWELS

ENDCAP
EYE HOLE

10. Wrap several paper towels around the mirrors so that when you slip the three mirrors into the canister, they fit snugly. Slide the mirror assemblage down the canister until it touches the eyepiece.

11. Put the open end of the canister on the clear, semirigid plastic and trace around the edge of the canister. Cut out the plastic disk. Trim it so that it fits snugly inside the open end of the canister and push it into the canister so that it rests on the ends of the mirrors. Using a few small pieces of tape, tape the disk to the inside of the canister.

12. Put some of the small, colorful objects on top of the plastic disk. Put the other end cap on. Look through the eyepiece at a sunny window (but not directly at the sun), turn the canister, and watch the changing patterns. You've made a replica of the first kaleidoscope!

Answers from the Past

David Brewster was a child prodigy who entered the University of Edinburgh in 1793 at age 12. His parents decided he should study to be a minister. He was ordained when he was 19 years old, but when he had to preach his first sermon, he discovered he was terrified of public speaking. He quickly changed his career for his real love, the study of optics.

I f you stand facing a rising or setting sun and look at a body of calm water, your eyes will be struck by glare, which is sunlight partially polarized by bouncing off the water at an angle. If you've ever worn polarized sunglasses, you know that they help reduce this glare. Polarized sunglass lenses are made in a way that blocks light traveling at particular angles.

Polarized lenses won't help you when you look straight down into the water. In that instance, most of the sun's rays that enter your eyes arrive head on. Polarized lenses can't block these rays.

Optics was a young science in the early 1800s, and there were many unanswered questions about the nature of light. In 1808, a young French scientist, Étienne Louis Malus, discovered that light could be **polarized** (made to travel in one plane) by reflecting it off a shiny surface. (Ordinarily, light travels out from its source in all planes.) Brewster read Malus's work and figured out the math for exactly how reflective surfaces polarize light.

While experimenting with polarized light materials, Brewster happened upon the phenomenon that underlies the kaleidoscope. Some scientists wouldn't have paid much attention to the beautiful effects produced by the two shiny pieces of metal, but Brewster did. He was a superb theoretical scientist, but he also loved the hands-on side of science and enjoyed building scientific instruments.

Brewster first experimented with changing the angle of the two mirrors where they joined, and discovered that he could change the number of reflections by changing the angle. Then, he realized that he got the most vivid effects by placing the viewing objects as close as possible to one end of the mirrors and holding the mirrors as close to his eye as possible.

At first, Brewster glued bits of colored glass to the end of the mirrors. One day, though, he hit on the idea of attaching a box at the end of the mirrors that could hold loose objects. That change allowed him to add motion to his device. Finally, using the telescope as a model, he attached the mirrors to the inside of a tube and added an eyepiece. At this point, he named his instrument the **kaleidoscope,** which means "beautiful form viewer" in Greek.

Brewster guessed that his kaleidoscope might make an amusing toy, and he was right. Kaleidoscopes became a fad, like hula hoops in the 1950s and Beanie Babies in the 1990s. Unfortunately, Brewster never made a penny from his invention. His device was copied and manufactured by others before he could patent it.

While he never made any money from his kaleidoscope, Brewster accomplished much in his life. He authored over 2,000 papers on optics and other subjects, wrote several biographies, invented other professional optical devices, became a member of the Royal Society (an association of the top scientists in Great Britain), and was knighted in 1832. He also invented a popular toy called a *stereoscope*, which allowed a viewer to look at two pictures of the same object at the same time (one through each eye), making the object appear to be three-dimensional.

INVENTOR'S CHALLENGE

Take the black cover off the third mirror in your kaleidoscope and see how images change. Untape the mirror assemblage and change the angle at which the mirrors meet. What is the maximum number of reflected images you can create? Can you redesign your kaleidoscope so that you can keep changing the angle of the mirrors as you look through the eyepiece?

3 Phenakistiscope

The Problem

You are a scientist in Belgium in 1830. You have studied how the eye receives an image and how the brain processes the information that the eye sends to it. You have been pondering the fact that when you blink your eyes, you don't see black. In fact, usually you are unaware that you've blinked: the image is uninterrupted. This phenomenon is called **persistence of vision,** which means that your brain briefly retains an image even after the image is no longer there. You have been trying to determine exactly how long the brain holds an image after it is gone.

It occurs to you that you could use the persistence of vision phenomenon to create the illusion of motion out of a series of still images. But how?

Observations

In 1825, Dr. John Ayrton Paris, a London doctor, patented the **thaumatrope,** a very simple toy that used the principle of persistence of vision. Dr. Paris cut out a small, round wooden disk that had a picture of a bird on one side and a picture of a birdcage on the other. He attached short pieces of string to opposite sides of the disk, pulled them taut, and then rotated the disk many times in one direction, thereby twisting the strings. When he released the disk, it spun rapidly in the opposite direction. Because of persistence of vision, anyone observing the spinning thaumatrope would see one image of a bird in a birdcage instead of two separate images.

The thaumatrope gives you an idea . . .

Materials

10-inch (25-cm)-diameter plate, bowl, or other
  circular object
heavy cardboard
pencil
scissors
ruler
photocopy of the drawings below
glue
thumbtack
wooden dowel
mirror attached to a wall

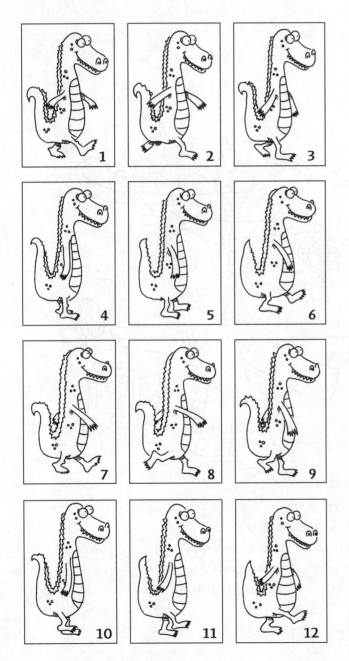

Experiment

1. Place the plate or bowl on the cardboard. Draw a circle by tracing around the edge of the plate or bowl. Cut out the disk.

2. With your ruler, draw a line through the center of the disk so that the disk is divided into two equal semicircles. Draw another line, perpendicular to the first, so that the disk is divided into four equal triangles. Draw lines that divide each triangle into three smaller triangles.

3. Where each line meets the edge of the disk, cut a slot that is 1 inch (2.5 cm) long and ⅛ to ¼ inch (about .5 cm) wide, as shown.

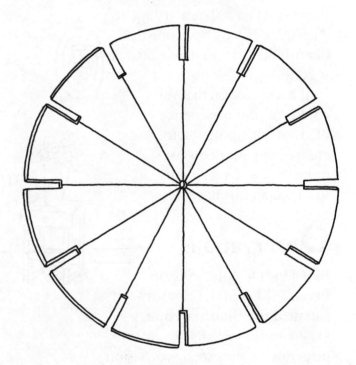

4. Cut out the drawings you copied on the lines. Glue the drawings, in numerical order, to the cardboard disk. The drawings should be centered between the slots, and the bottoms of the drawings should be about ½ inch (1 cm) below the bottom of the slots.

5. Push the thumbtack through the center of the front of the disk. Push the tack into the side of the dowel near the top.

6. Hold the dowel so that the disk faces the mirror. Stand behind the disk so that you see its reflection in the mirror, as shown.

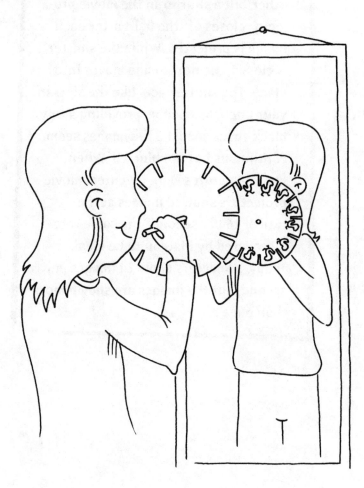

7. Spin the disk and look through the slits at the mirror. (You may need to widen the hole where the thumbtack attaches the disk to the dowel a bit if the disk doesn't spin well.) You should see a "movie" in the mirror!

Answers from the Past

Joseph Antoine Ferdinand Plateau was a mathematician, physicist, chemist, and inventor born in Belgium in 1801. His father was an artist, and he sent Joseph to art school in hopes that his son would follow in his footsteps. However, Plateau became more interested in the physiology of optics—that is, how the brain physically receives and perceives images. He studied to become a scientist and received his doctorate in physics from the University of Ghent in Belgium. In the early 1830s, he focused his attention on the phenomenon of persistence of vision, which scientists had observed, but no one had studied carefully.

Plateau measured persistence of vision and discovered that the brain retains an image of an object for about 1/30 of a second after the image has been removed. That may not seem like a long time, but it is about as long as it takes you to blink.

Plateau also discovered that when the eye and the brain are presented with a series of images, they need a rest between the images. Without a rest or black space between them, the images overlap each other in the brain and turn into a blur. (That's why you made slits in the disk. Make another copy of the images and glue them on a disk without slits and see for yourself what happens when you don't get a break between images.) If the rest between images is too long, though, the brain perceives the blank space between the images and the motion sequence is jerky or flickers.

Plateau used his knowledge to invent the **phenakistiscope** (which in Greek means "a cheating device for viewing") in 1832. He used it and other devices to further study how the brain reacts when presented with a series of images. Through his phenakistiscope experiments, Plateau realized that there is an ideal number of images per second separated by a tiny black space that makes the brain perceive continuous motion from a series of still images. He discovered that 16 images per second is that ideal number.

After Plateau patented his phenakistiscope in 1832, he also discovered that it was a very popular toy. Other inventors developed devices that improved on the phenakistiscope. In 1834, William George Horner invented the **zoetrope,** which had the pictures lining a rotating drum. In 1876, Emile Reynaud, a Frenchman, painted the images onto strips of celluloid, an early plastic, and projected the images with mirrors onto a screen. Thomas Edison invented a hand-cranked projector, called a **kinetoscope,** in 1891. The kinetoscope moved a strip of film in front of a light source and lens and projected the images on a small screen in a booth. In 1906, J. Stuart Blackton put together the insights of Plateau, Reynaud, and Edison to create the first animated cartoon film, *Humorous Phases of Funny Faces.*

INVENTOR'S CHALLENGE

Make your own action sequences for a phenakistiscope. See what happens if you also put images on the disk below the slots. Try creating a sequence where your images gradually change colors.

On a piece of movie film, the images are right next to each other, but a shutter in the movie projector closes off the light after each image is projected. While the shutter is closed, the next image moves into place. The shutter acts like the slots in your phenakistiscope, providing a tiny black space to make the images seem continuous but not blurred. When motion pictures were invented, movie projectors showed images at the rate of 16 per second—the same rate discovered by Plateau to be ideal. Today, projectors show 24 images per second, but the images are shown more than once.

4 Periscope

The Problem

It is 1902, and you are Simon Lake, the American inventor of the world's first practical submarine. You have tried to interest the U.S. Navy in buying your submarines, but have never been successful. Fortunately, your subs are well adapted for other uses, and you have made millions of dollars salvaging treasure and cargo from wrecks off the coast of the eastern United States.

In the past few years, underwater torpedoes launched from surface ships have become an effective way of sinking enemy vessels. People are now suggesting that torpedoes would be even more effective if launched from a submarine. A submarine hidden beneath the surface would have a greater chance of surprising the enemy with a torpedo attack.

There is one problem with this proposal. To position a sub for an accurate torpedo attack, you must be able to see the target at fairly close range. But even on a calm day, you can't see more than a few yards underwater through portholes. You would have to bring the top of the sub above the surface so that the viewing portholes of the **conning tower** (the low, broad tower on top of the sub

FIRE!

used for observation and entry) were out of the water. But then the enemy might see you and torpedo you first.

The U.S. Navy is requesting bids for a new submarine design to be used to launch torpedoes. How can you fix your sub so that the people inside can see the enemy without the enemy seeing the sub?

Observations

You know John Holland, your rival at Electric Boat Company, has been experimenting with a kind of **camera lucida** (a lens and mirror system that artists have long used), which projects an image of the enemy ship onto a piece of paper. Holland has mounted the device in a long, vertical tube that projects out of the top of the sub. Holland's device is not terribly useful: it captures a still image and doesn't allow you to gauge the distance to the ship. Still, some elements of his device give you an idea . . .

MATERIALS
poster board
ruler
pencil
scissors
tape
two 4-inch (10-cm)-diameter round or square mirrors

Experiment

1. Measure and cut a 10- × 20-inch (25- × 50-cm) rectangle on the poster board.

2. Bend the rectangle into a long tube, overlapping the edges by about 1 inch (2.5 cm). Tape the seam closed. This is your periscope tube.

3. Place the tube on a table with its seam facing to the left. On the outside of the end

of the tube nearest you, measure 3 inches (7.5 cm) from the edge and make a mark.

4. Roll the tube so that the seam faces right. On the outside of the end of the tube farthest from you, measure 3 inches (7.5 cm) from the edge and make a mark.

5. Cut from the mark on an angle to the end of the opposite side of the tube and back at the same angle to the mark. You will be cutting off the end of the tube at a 45° angle.

6. Repeat on the other end of the tube.

7. Each end of the tube now has a short and a long side. From the long side of each end, measure 2 inches (5 cm) and make a mark. Draw a 2-inch (5-cm)-diameter circle around the mark. Cut out the circles, as shown.

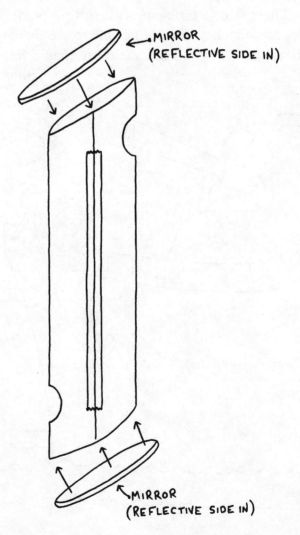

MIRROR (REFLECTIVE SIDE IN)

MIRROR (REFLECTIVE SIDE IN)

8. Tape a mirror over each end of the tube so that the reflective sides of the mirrors face into the tube.

9. Sit in front of a table, facing the table so that your face is below the edge. Hold the periscope so that when you look into one hole, the hole at the other end is above the table top. With your periscope, you should be able to see what's going on above the surface of the table when you're below it! Think of other ways to use your periscope to see things while you remain hidden.

Answers from the Past

Simon Lake built his first submarine, the *Argonaut Junior*, in 1895 when he was 28 years old. His sub looked like a huge wedge of cheese 14½ feet (4.5 meters) long, 4½ feet (1.3 meters) wide at the back end, pointed at the front end, and 5 feet (1.5 meters) high. It was made of thin pine boards and had wooden wheels so that it could roll across an ocean or river floor. Two divers fit inside and turned the wheels with hand cranks.

Lake rapidly improved his first design, and by 1898, he had built a 56-foot (17-meter)-long steel submarine that was able to make a 2-month, 1,000-mile (1,600-km) trip up the Atlantic coast, staying underwater for as long as 24 hours. Although Lake tried to interest the U.S. Navy in his designs, his competitor, John Holland, secured whatever government contracts were available. Lake turned his attention to salvaging shipwrecks, making a fortune in the process.

Until about 1902, Lake and others believed that naval submarines were best used to secretly transport divers so that they could place bombs beneath enemy ships or cut their anchor cables. Two inventions changed the role of the

A mirror produces images by reflecting light. If you hold a *plane mirror* (meaning a flat mirror) parallel to an object, it will reflect the light bouncing off the object directly back at it. That is why when you look directly into a mirror, you see yourself.

When light reaches a plane mirror, it bounces off the mirror at that same angle, but in the opposite direction. (You can see how this works by rolling a rubber ball at a wall at different angles.) In your periscope experiment, you place the mirrors at 45° angles. So, rays of light coming from the room reflect off the mirror at the top of the periscope at a 45° angle, or directly down toward the bottom of the periscope. The mirror at the bottom reflects the light again, also at a 45° angle, directly toward your eye. The image of the room is bent twice before it gets to your eye.

submarine in warfare. One was the Whitehead torpedo, which was propelled by a compressed-air engine and could launch 18 pounds (8 kilos) of dynamite at enemy ships from a distance. The other was Lake's periscope.

Before the periscope (from the Greek for "to look around"), submariners navigated by compass underwater and surfaced frequently to figure out exactly where they were. Once Lake invented the periscope, the submarine became an important offensive weapon. A submarine captain projected a slender, nearly invisible periscope above the water's surface, positioned his sub so that its torpedo tubes were in line with the target ship, and fired—all from a safe distance.

INVENTOR'S CHALLENGE

Your periscope allows you to see what is in front of you. You could, of course, turn yourself and the periscope around to see what's behind you. But can you alter your periscope so that you can sit still and see all around you?

Hint: Get out your scissors.

Notice something funny about what you see when you look directly behind you with your modified periscope? Draw a diagram of how the light from the top and bottom of the object you're looking at hits the two mirrors and then your eye. Do you understand why you see this odd phenomenon?

More than 200 years before the periscope was invented, some fashionable theater-goers brought a little device called a *polemoscope* to performances. The polemoscope looked like a monocular (binoculars for one eye) for viewing the performers on stage. But the polemoscope didn't have a working lens at the front. Instead, it had a hole in its side. Inside the tube, there was a plane mirror set at a 45° angle to the hole. When you looked into the polemoscope, people would think you were looking at the stage, but instead you were looking to the side. This way you could watch someone else in the seats beside you. You can see why another name for the polemoscope was the "jealousy glass!"

PART II

Inventions That Move Through Air and Water

Humans have never been satisfied with the physical limitations of their finless, wingless bodies. It would seem, however, that traveling through air or water would be impossible for us. In fact, our species has devoted a great deal of inventive creativity over the millennia to conquering these limitations. Today we can move, with the help of our inventions, much faster through water and air than any creature naturally designed to swim or fly.

The first artificial means of transportation was the boat. All over the globe, ancient people observed floating logs and reeds, and experimented with binding them together to make rafts. Rafts floating on top of water inspired people to build more seaworthy boats that sat deeper in the water and cut through it with sleek hulls. In the twentieth century, as you will see, Christopher Cockerell took boats in a new direction when he invented the hovercraft, which used a blast of air to float a ship above the water.

Air travel developed much later, but quickly. The Montgolfier brothers took the first step in 1783 when they sent two passengers aloft in a hot air balloon. The parachute came next in 1797. Sir George Cayley started experimenting with fixed-wing aircraft in 1853 when he put his coachman in a glider and pushed him off to a 1,640-foot (500-meter) flight across a valley. (The Aerobie that you'll reinvent uses principles first explored by Cayley.) In 1903, the Wright brothers made the first engine-powered, fixed-wing flight. Only 23 years later, Robert Goddard sent the first liquid-fueled rocket, predecessor of the rockets that lift the space shuttle, toward space.

5 Hulled Sailboat

The Problem

You are the owner of a sailing raft on the Nile River in Egypt in 6000 B.C. Your raft is made of long bundles of the reeds called papyrus that grow all along the shore of the Nile. It is easy to take people and their goods north on the river. The Nile flows from south to north, so you simply float along with the current, using a pole for steering. To travel south, though, you have put up your square sail to catch the *bai,* the wind that often blows from the north to the south.

The gods have arranged the wind and the current very well, in your opinion, for traveling the Nile, but there are a few problems with your sailing raft. The biggest problem is that your raft is hard to steer, especially sailing south. When the wind is directly behind you, all is well and you travel in a straight line. But if the wind comes a little from the side, your raft slips sideways.

What can you do to solve this problem?

Observations

When you put a heavy load on a narrow raft, you notice that the raft sits more deeply in the water. That makes the raft easier to steer in a straight line, but it also means everyone and everything on the raft gets wet!

MATERIALS

scissors

ruler

2-inch (5-cm)-wide clear packing tape

wire cutter

six 18-inch (45-cm) paper-covered, wire flower stems (available at craft stores or florist shops)

pencil

corrugated cardboard

transparent tape

pea-sized ball of modeling clay

piece of copier paper

¼ cup (50 ml) uncooked rice

Experiment

1. Cut a 12-inch (30-cm) piece of packing tape. Place it, sticky side up, on a table. Cut another 12-inch (30-cm) piece of packing tape. Place it so that the long edge of the second piece overlaps the long edge of the first piece by about ¼ inch (½ cm). Repeat with a third piece of packing tape.

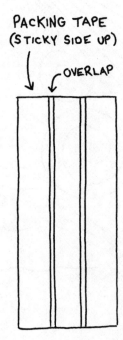

PACKING TAPE (STICKY SIDE UP)

OVERLAP

2. Use the wire cutter to cut the flower stems in half. Put a pencil mark 1 inch (2.5 cm) from both ends of each of ten stems. Bend the stems at the pencil mark at about 45°.

3. You will see that the cardboard is a sandwich of two flat pieces of paper with a piece of folded paper in between. The piece of paper inside forms long tubes. The tubes are much like the hollow reeds of the papyrus plant. Cut a 2- × 7½-inch (2.5- × 19-cm) piece of corrugated cardboard so that the long sides of the piece are parallel with the tubes.

4. Bend the piece of cardboard lengthwise along the "reeds" so that the cardboard is bent into a shallow **U** shape. This is the bottom of your reed sailboat.

5. Center the cardboard on the tape so that the outer curve of the **U** is against the tape. Press the sides of the tape up against the sides of the **U**, as shown.

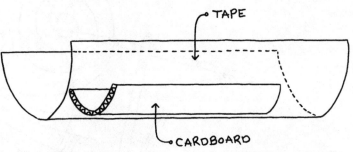

TAPE

CARDBOARD

6. Roll the bottom of the boat a little to one side so that the tape on one side is flat on the table, as shown. Place one of the flower stems next to one long side of the cardboard so that the bent ends point up. Press it against the tape so that it sticks in place. Place four more stems next to the first one. Roll the bottom of the boat to the other side, and repeat to place five stems in the same way on the tape on this side.

7. Push up the two sides of the packing tape with the stems on them so that they are parallel to each other. The bent ends of the stems will come together to form the **bow** (the front) and the **stern** (the back) of the boat. Fold the tape over the sides of the boat. Fold the tape over the bent ends to hold them in place. Trim the excess tape that sticks up off the bow and stern.

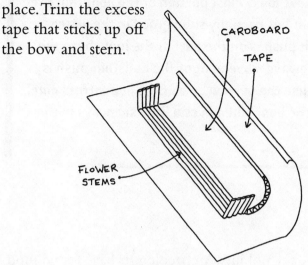

CAROBOARD

TAPE

FLOWER STEMS

8. About 2 inches (5 cm) from the bow, put a piece of transparent tape across the top of the sides, as shown. Put two more pieces of tape on top of the first piece. Cut a ½-inch (1-cm) slit lengthwise in the tape. Put the small ball of modeling clay beneath the tape and push it firmly onto the floor of the boat.

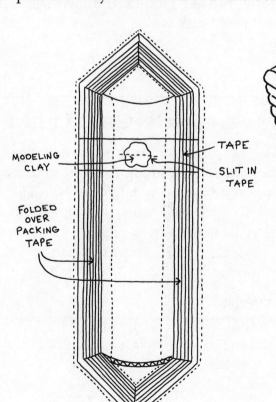

MODELING CLAY

TAPE

SLIT IN TAPE

FOLDED OVER PACKING TAPE

9. Cut the two remaining stems to a 6-inch (15-cm) length. One inch (2.5 cm) from the end of one stem, bend the stem to form a right (90°) angle. Repeat with the other stem. Hold the two stems together so that they form a T, as shown. Tape them together just below the bar of the T. Cut a 3-inch (7.5-cm) square of paper. Tape the top edge of the square to the bar of the T. The two stems are your mast and the paper is your sail.

10. Stick the mast through the hole in the tape into the modeling clay, as shown. Make sure the mast is centered (from right to left) in the boat. You've made an ancient Egyptian hulled sailboat—perhaps the first hulled sailboat in the world!

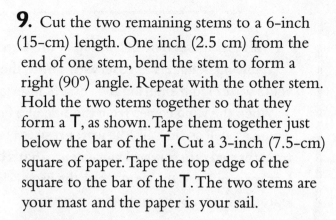

11. Spread the rice evenly in the bottom of the boat. Put a few inches of water in a sink or bathtub. Put your hulled sailboat in the water. (You may need to adjust the mast so that it doesn't tip your boat.) Blow gently on the sail from the stern and see it sail away. Try blowing on the sail from a position not directly behind the boat. Notice that your boat still moves forward.

A raft is a vessel that sits on top of the water. It tends to move in the direction the wind is blowing. A boat is a vessel with a **hull**, the hollow, lowermost portion of the boat that prevents water from entering the vessel's interior. A hull is partially submerged in the water.

When the wind comes from the side of a boat, it pushes on the part of the hull above the water, as well as the sail. The water resists the sideways movement of the hull; that push is transformed into forward movement. That's because the narrow bow of the boat offers much less resistance to the water than the broad side. The boat still moves a little sideways in the water, but most of its motion is forward.

Answers from the Past

Sometime early in the third millennium B.C., the ancient Egyptians began to switch from flat sailing rafts to boats made of reeds bundled and tied together to form a hull. To prevent water from seeping in between the bundles of reeds, they covered the outside of the boat with **pitch** (a gooey black substance made from tar or petroleum).

Hulled sailboats were often portrayed on ancient Egyptian murals, and they appear to have been used primarily for hunting and for pleasure by the nobility. Archaeologists have found models of them in the tombs of Egyptian royalty. The boats were well suited for traveling on the calm Nile, but were less useful on the open sea.

Reed rafts and reed boats were made all along the coast of the Mediterranean Sea. They were also made by Native American tribes in South America. Today, Aymara Indians who live along the banks of Lake Titicaca in Bolivia still make and sail reed boats.

Some people believe that Egyptians may have sailed on reed boats across the Atlantic Ocean to South America. In the early 1970s, Norwegian Thor Heyerdahl built a large reed sailboat with the help of Bolivian Aymara Indians and sailed from Egypt to Barbados, an island in the Caribbean Sea. The *Ra II*, as the boat was called, sailed 4,000 miles in 57 days. Heyerdahl proved that a transatlantic voyage could have taken place, but there is no evidence that it actually did.

INVENTOR'S CHALLENGE

The Egyptian sailboats worked well when the wind was coming from behind the boat, as it most often did on the Nile. They didn't work well when the wind came from the side. Can you improve the design of the sail to make a boat that sails well in a crosswind?

Materials

scissors   stiff plastic
paper   tape
string

6 Parachute

The Problem

You are André Jacques Garnerin, a soldier in the French army in 1795, and, to your great regret, you find yourself a prisoner of war in a castle-like fortress in Bade, Hungary. Before enlisting in the French army, you studied physics and were on your way to a career flying the huge gas balloons that the Montgolfier brothers invented in 1783. Now, lonely and homesick in the fortress of Bade, you start thinking about ways to escape. Naturally, your thoughts turn to flight. Getting a balloon and the hot air or hydrogen gas to fill it is impossible, but maybe there is another way to float out of your prison. You start making some calculations . . .

Observations

You have heard about a fellow French balloon enthusiast, Jean Pierre Blanchard, who had experimented with what the newspaper described as a "falling screen." In his experiments, Blanchard put up a small hydrogen balloon tethered by a rope to the ground. Beneath the balloon hung a basket with a dog inside. When a fuse automatically released the basket from the balloon, it also released a screen, and the basket and animal descended to earth, suspended beneath the screen.

You have also heard about another inventive Frenchman, Louis-Sebastien Lenormand. Lenormand constructed a 14-foot (4.3-meter) umbrella-like device, which he used to jump safely out of the window of a tall house. Lenormand promoted his device as a way to escape a burning building.

MATERIALS

six pieces of 8- × 11-inch (20- × 28-cm) tissue paper
pencil
scissors
glue
thread
transparent tape
small paper or plastic cup

Experiment

1. Photocopy or trace Pattern A and cut it out. Make a stack of the six pieces of tissue paper. Trace Pattern A onto the top layer of tissue paper. Cut out six pieces all at once.

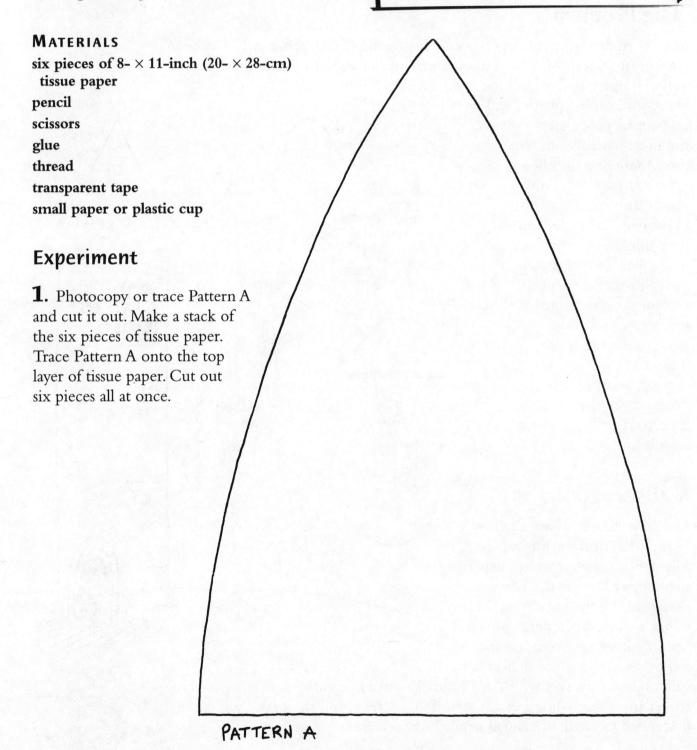

PATTERN A

2. Place a thin smear of glue along one of the long, curved edges of one piece of tissue paper. Glue it to a long edge of another piece so that they overlap about ¼ inch (½ cm). This can be tricky because you are piecing together a three-dimensional object. As you overlap the pieces, curve them. Don't worry about a few wrinkles or a little hole or if the overlap isn't even.

3. Glue a third piece of tissue paper to the first two. Continue gluing until all six pieces are glued together to form a hemisphere. This is your parachute canopy. Let it dry.

4. Cut six pieces of thread 14 inches (35 cm) long. Use a small piece of tape to tape one end of a thread to the bottom of a canopy seam. Repeat with the other five threads.

5. Cut the cup to a height of about 2 inches (5 cm). Tape the other end of the threads to the outside edge of the cup. Tape the thread to the cup at

regular intervals and make sure that no strings cross, as shown.

6. Hold your parachute by the top of its canopy and as high off the ground as you safely can (you might want to climb on a chair or table). Let go. You've made a replica of the world's first parachute!

A parachute works by taking advantage of friction between the parachute's canopy and air. (**Friction** is a force that slows down a moving object that is in contact with a gas, liquid, or solid.) Without a parachute, a person dropped from a balloon is pulled to earth by gravity at an accelerating rate to a speed of over 100 miles (160 km) per hour. When a parachute opens, the large surface of its canopy encounters and pulls through the molecules of gas (primarily nitrogen and oxygen) in our atmosphere. This friction slows a parachutist to about 14 miles (22.5 km) per hour. Landing at that speed will give you a jolt, but a parachutist learns how to land safely.

Answers from the Past

The two Montgolfier brothers invented the hot air balloon in France in 1783. Their first balloons were made of canvas and filled with hot air. Because hot air is lighter than cold air, their balloons rose. As the air inside cooled, the balloons gently descended. A young Frenchman named André Jacques Garnerin took his first balloon flight in 1787, and instantly became a balloon enthusiast.

Ballooning was the rage at the end of the eighteenth century. Watching the beautifully colored balloons rise and glide through the air became a popular entertainment, and balloonists were able to make a living demonstrating balloons at public fairs and celebrations. Balloonists soon replaced their hot air balloons with balloons filled with hydrogen gas. Hot air balloons fell and rose as the air inside them cooled and was reheated, which made them hard to control. Because hydrogen gas maintained a relatively constant upward thrust on the balloon, a hydrogen balloon's behavior was more predictable and easier to control.

Garnerin was on his way to becoming a professional balloonist when the French Revolution of 1789 interrupted his career. He joined the French army, where he promoted the use of balloons as military tools. In 1793, Garnerin was taken prisoner, and found himself in a fortress prison camp in Hungary. He dreamed of escaping by air, but knew he couldn't get the hydrogen or the means of making hot air in prison. He began to design a device that looked like the top half of a balloon, which he thought might float him down to freedom.

Garnerin never had the chance to test his design in prison because he was released from captivity in 1795. Two years later, he completed the design and construction of a silk parachute that looked much like your tissue paper model. On October 22, 1797, he went up in a hot air balloon to a height of about 3,000 feet (1,000 meters, or roughly twice the height of the Empire State Building). He climbed from the large basket (called a *gondola*) beneath his balloon and into another basket about the size of a modern garbage can, which was attached by a rope to the side of the gondola. He cut the rope, and, of course, fell like a rock. After a few seconds, though, the 30-foot (10-meter)-wide canopy of his parachute opened, and his fall slowed dramatically. Garnerin, suspended in his basket, rocked wildly from side to side, like a pendulum gone mad. The spectators below feared for his safety, but he landed with only a sprained ankle.

A modern twist on the parachute is the *parafoil*. A parafoil is made of lightweight fabric that is shaped like a large, curved rectangle. The rectangular fabric is attached by cords to a person hanging below. The particular shape of the rectangle is important because the parafoil acts like an airplane wing. A parafoil counters the power of gravity not only through air resistance, but also through **lift**. Lift is an upward force that is created by the difference in air pressure above and below a curved wing as the wing moves through the air.

Garnerin earned his living as a balloonist and a parachutist. He discovered that if he put a hole in the very top of the canopy, the parachute dropped without rocking. (The hole allows a little air to escape smoothly, reducing the turbulence around the edges of the parachute.) Garnerin's wife and niece joined him in his business, and they performed as a family across Europe.

INVENTOR'S CHALLENGE

Can you safely land an uncooked egg by parachute (or parachutes)? From what height? Change the design of your parachute or its materials as you wish. Perhaps your egg will need some cushioning. . . . And you might want to make your early tests with a hard-boiled egg! (*Caution:* Always wash your hands after handling raw eggs. They may contain harmful bacteria.)

7 | Liquid-Fueled Rocket

The Problem

It's 1925 in Massachusetts, and space travel is decades in the future. You are an imaginative inventor, though, and know that the first step to making space travel a reality is to get beyond earth's atmosphere.

You know you can't fly an airplane into space because space is a **vacuum**—there's no air there. An airplane depends on the difference in air pressure above and below a plane's wings to make it fly. Also, a plane's propellers won't work in space because they need to push air to work. You wonder: Can you invent a vehicle that doesn't need the presence of air to fly?

Observations

You've seen what happens when you blow up a balloon with air, pinch its neck closed, and then remove your fingers. The air inside (a mix of nitrogen, oxygen, and other gases), which is under pressure, rushes out and sends the balloon across the room. You've shaken a bottle of soda water (water with carbon dioxide gas dissolved in it) and then removed the bottle top: a spray of carbon dioxide gas and soda shot out. You know that when gases expand out of an enclosed space, they can do so with powerful force.

MATERIALS
baking soda
coffee filter
water
white vinegar
clean, empty 1-liter plastic soda bottle
adult helper
cork that fits snugly in the top of the bottle

Experiment

1. Go outside to do this experiment.

2. Put 4 teaspoons (20 ml) of baking soda in the coffee filter. Wrap up the baking soda in the filter and twist the ends of the filter as tightly as possible.

3. Pour ½ cup (125 ml) of water and ½ cup (125 ml) of vinegar into the soda bottle.

4. Ask your adult helper to have the cork ready. Slip the coffee filter into the bottle and hand the bottle to your adult helper. Have your helper quickly push the cork snugly into the bottle top. Put the bottle on the ground, and stand way back. *Make sure the bottle does not point at anyone: the cork will come out fast!* You've

---

What makes the cork blast off? Vinegar and baking soda combine to make carbon dioxide gas—the same gas that makes your soda fizz. As the vinegar and baking soda combine, carbon dioxide fills—and then overfills—the bottle. The gas can't push out the rigid walls of the bottle, but it can push out through the top, propelling the cork with it.

Real rockets don't combine vinegar and baking soda, of course, but they combine other liquid and solid fuels. A rocket has a **combustion chamber** (like your plastic bottle). In the combustion chamber, chemical fuels are combined and react to produce hot gases. The hot gases exit through nozzles in the bottom of the combustion chamber with enough force to send the rocket straight up through the air into space.

made a liquid-fueled rocket! (If the cork doesn't take off, ask your adult helper to push the cork in more tightly the next time.)

Answers from the Past

Robert Goddard was a 16-year-old American high school student in 1899 when he first dreamed about space travel. He realized that a device that could fly through the blanket of air above the earth and escape the pull of earth's gravity would have to have a new form and a new fuel. Goddard continued to work in college on the puzzle of how to get into space, became a professor of physics, and spent his career experimenting with rockets.

When Goddard started his work, he first looked at other devices that might give him inspiration. He took apart Chinese fireworks as well as signal flares that sent bright colored sparks high in the air. (The Chinese developed fireworks in about 1250.) He inspected military rockets that launched explosives. All of these devices used the explosive force of gunpowder to launch them, but Goddard soon realized that gunpowder couldn't send a rocket into space.

Gunpowder burns all at once, and a rocket needs a continuous push over the course of about 150 miles to space. Still, the design of these devices gave him ideas for a space rocket.

Did you notice that the baking soda and vinegar did not react all at once? The "fuels" reacted over a period of time, providing a steady source of power for the cork, not just a one-time burst.

Goddard considered fuels other than gunpowder. Scientists at the time used helium balloons to lift barometers and other measuring devices into the upper atmosphere. So, Goddard considered sending a rocket up on a balloon and then launching it when it was high above the Earth. He also considered using solar (the sun's) energy. Neither of these methods turned out to be practical.

Even though using helium balloons didn't work out, Goddard's idea to launch objects from a place above the Earth's surface was a good one. Almost all of a rocket's fuel is used to escape Earth's atmosphere. In 1989, NASA used the space shuttle, which orbits 160 miles above the Earth, to launch *Galileo*, a spacecraft that investigated the planet Jupiter.

Ultimately, Goddard realized that a fuel made of liquid oxygen and liquid hydrogen was the best way to power a rocket to space. These fuels were expensive, though, and hard to use. (Liquid oxygen has to be kept colder than −297°F

[−148°C] to stay liquid. Hydrogen must be cooled to −423°F [−253°C].) Finding the right fuel wasn't the only problem Goddard had to solve. He had to invent fuel pumps and steering systems for his rockets. He also had to invent a cooling system for the rocket's combustion chamber so that fuels—burning at 4,000°F (2,222°C)—wouldn't burn through the chamber's walls.

Robert Goddard launched his first liquid-fueled rocket in 1926 on his aunt's farm in Massachusetts. The rocket was 10½ feet (3.2 meters) tall, weighed 10 pounds (4.5 kg), and used liquid oxygen and gasoline as fuel. Goddard's assistant lit the rocket's engine with a blowtorch. It took over a minute for the fuels to produce enough gas to lift the rocket slowly off the ground. The rocket accelerated to about 60 miles per hour (100 km per hour) and reached an altitude of 41 feet (12.6 meters), or the height of a four-story building. The flight time was only 2.5 seconds, but the space age had begun.

Goddard worked his whole life on solving rocketry problems, and launched hundreds of experimental rockets. The U.S. Patent Office granted him over 200 patents on devices related to rocketry. When he died in 1945, he hadn't yet launched a rocket that made it into space, but his work was essential to later space explorations. When the first satellites were launched into space (the Russian satellite, *Sputnik,* in 1957 and the

American satellite, *Explorer,* in 1958), both were riding rockets that were direct descendants of Goddard's rockets.

Dr. Robert Goddard and his liquid-fuel rocket (Courtesy of NASA).

INVENTOR'S CHALLENGE

Can you invent a vinegar–and–baking soda–powered boat using the soda bottle?

CLUE
A straw may come in handy.

8 | Hovercraft

The Problem

It's 1950, and you're an engineer who has just started a boat-building business on the western coast of England. You're also an inventor, so you start thinking about ways to make your boats faster. You know that the amount of friction (**drag**) of the water against a boat's hull is important in determining a boat's speed. The less of the hull that contacts the water, the faster the boat can go.

You begin to wonder if you could design a boat that has no drag at all. Would it be possible to eliminate the contact between the hull and the water completely?

Observations

You've read about Sir John Thornycroft, an English inventor in the 1870s who tried to design and build a boat that rode along on a cushion of air forced downward beneath the hull. Thornycroft never succeeded, though, partly

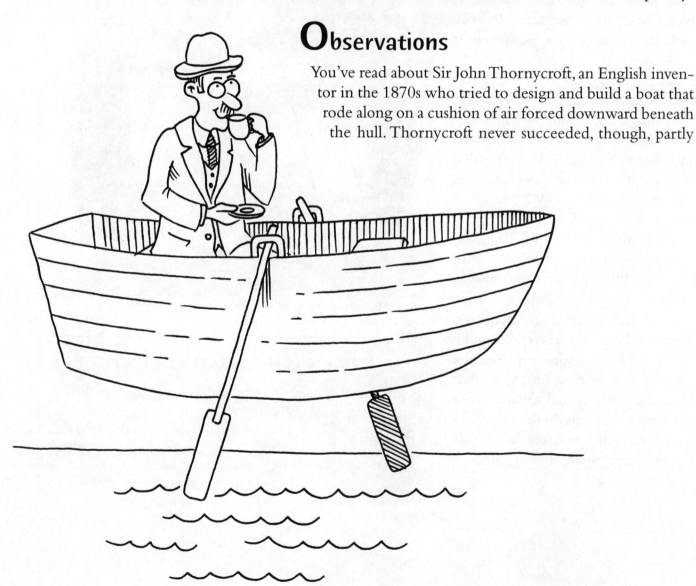

because there were no engines at the time that could produce a strong enough flow of air. He also couldn't figure out how to contain the air under the boat. But you have an idea . . .

MATERIALS

9- × 9-inch (23- × 23-cm) piece of foam core board (foam core board is a lightweight board made of two pieces of paper with a layer of Styrofoam inside)

compass

pencil

ruler

adult helper

scissors

¾-inch (2-cm) diameter plastic spool of thread

glue

piece of copier paper

12-inch (30-cm)-diameter balloon

Experiment

1. Place the piece of foam core board on a table. (If the board is not completely flat, hold it so that the edges curve up.) Use the compass to draw a 6-inch (15-cm)-diameter circle in the foam core board.

2. Cut out the disk.

3. Ask your adult helper to use the scissors to make a hole in the center of the disk. The hole in the disk should be the same size as the hole in the spool of thread.

4. Spread glue all over one end of the spool. Press the glued end onto the top side of the disk so that the holes in the spool and in the disk line up.

5. Cut a circle of paper to cover the hole at the other end of the spool. Glue the circle to the other end of the spool.

6. Let the glue on both ends dry thoroughly. After the glue is dry, use your pencil to put a ⅛-inch (.3-cm) hole in the paper covering.

7. Blow up the balloon and twist the end so that the air can't escape. While you hold the twist of the balloon, have your helper stretch the balloon over the end of the spool.

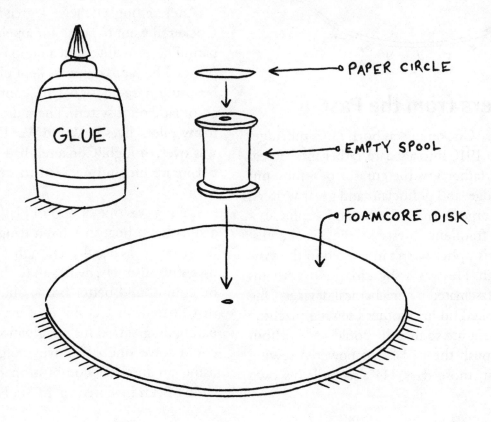

GLUE

PAPER CIRCLE

EMPTY SPOOL

FOAMCORE DISK

8. Put the disk on the tabletop and let go of the balloon. Your hovercraft should glide across the table. (If it doesn't, first try widening the hole in the paper covering on the spool. You can also try reducing the size of the disk.) Your hovercraft is riding on a cushion of air.

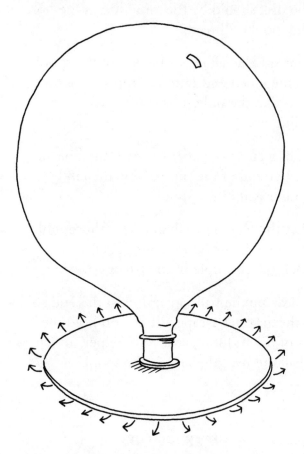

The one visitor who Cockerell took an interest in was T. E. Lawrence, otherwise known as Lawrence of Arabia—a famous adventurer, archaeologist, and writer—who let Christopher examine his powerful new motorcycle.

Answers from the Past

Christopher Cockerell was born in Cambridge, England, in 1910 into a sedate, rather intellectual family. His father was the curator of a museum in Cambridge, and politicians and great writers, such as George Bernard Shaw and Joseph Conrad, were frequent guests at the Cockerells' house. Christopher wasn't interested in the visitors, though. He was a shy kid, good with his hands and fascinated by mechanical devices. One day, he hooked up his mother's sewing machine to a steam engine so that she could sew without having to push the pedal that powered sewing machines in those days. He also built his own radios.

After getting a college degree in engineering, Cockerell went to work for an electronics company. There, he invented a radio compass for airplanes. The radio compass kept planes on course by using a radio signal to control the plane's automatic pilot system. The radio compass saved many pilots' lives in World War II. After the war was over, though, Cockerell had had enough of corporate life and decided to strike out on his own.

Sailing was one of his hobbies, and he bought a run-down boatyard, fixed it up, and began to build boats. Naturally enough for a man with inventive instincts, he began to think about how he could build better boats. The idea of a boat that floated on a cushion of air, thereby eliminating drag, seized his imagination. He knew he could solve one of Thornycroft's problems by using an internal combustion engine (which hadn't been invented in 1870). He then put his mind to solving the problem of containing the air beneath the boat.

In his first experiment, Cockerell used two empty tin cans, one slightly smaller than the other. He put the smaller can upside down inside the larger one, attached a blower, and blew air down the space between the two cans. The cylindrical curtain of air that rushed out the bottom of the cans easily lifted them off the ground.

Cockerell's design worked because engines on his hovercraft blasted air around the edge of the underside of his boat to create a high-pressure ring of air. The ring of air pushed the hull up and then circulated under the hull to keep it suspended. The ring of air also acted like an invisible curtain, keeping air under the hull from escaping. In 1962, hovercraft were improved by fitting them with flexible rubber skirts to further prevent air from escaping.

Cockerell went on to make a 2-foot (60-cm) model of what he called a "hovercraft."

Cockerell didn't have the money to build a full-scale model, but thought the British government would be interested in his invention. To make a memorable impression on government officials, he took his little hovercraft with him on a leash and let it wander around like a dog. In 1959, the government and a private company together produced the first hovercraft based on Cockerell's designs. Until the Chunnel (the tunnel beneath the English Channel that links England and France) was completed, hovercraft provided regular ferry service across the Channel.

Today, hovercraft are used by businesses to move people and goods across water and land. Some provide ferry service or sightseeing tours. There are also racing clubs for hovercraft!

INVENTOR'S CHALLENGE

Can you invent a way to make your hovercraft go in a particular direction?

9 Aerobie

The Problem

It is the early 1970s, and you are Alan Adler, an electronics engineer and an experienced designer of racing sailboats. At the moment, you are also frustrated. You like to play Frisbee with your friends, and it's very irritating that you can't throw a Frisbee very well. One day you pick up the Frisbee and look at it carefully. You wonder why you can't throw it farther. Maybe if you made a few design improvements . . .

Observations

As a sailboat designer, you are very familiar with the way air moves over curved surfaces (such as sails). Looking at the Frisbee, you notice that its edge is quite thick. Surely, a sleeker shape would fly farther through the air.

MATERIALS

drawing compass with a pencil

flat sheet of corrugated cardboard about 12
  inches (30 cm) square

adult helper

sharp craft knife

marker

Experiment

1. Place the pointed leg of your compass near the center of the cardboard square. Draw a circle with a 3½-inch (8.75-cm) radius. Keep the pointed leg in the same place. Draw a circle with a 4⅞-inch (12.2-cm) radius. Keep the pointed leg in the same place. Draw a circle with a 5-inch (12.5-cm) radius around the first circle.

2. Ask an adult helper to use the sharp craft knife to trim the cardboard away from the outermost circle and the innermost circle so that you are left with a ring. Don't crease the ring.

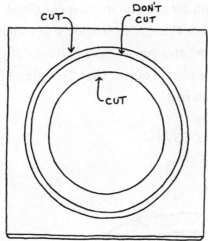

CUT

DON'T CUT

CUT

3. Mark one side of the ring "top" and the other side "bottom."

4. With the top side up, carefully bend the inside edge of the top surface of the ring up just a little bit. Work your way slowly around the top surface of the ring. When you finish, the inside of the ring should be just a little higher than the outside, as shown. (To see if you've got the right degree of bend, put the ring in your right hand and toss it like a Frisbee, parallel to the ground. If it curves to the right, flatten the bend a little. If it curves left, bend it a little more. It should fly straight, and then finally curve to the left as it reaches the ground.)

5. Ask your adult helper to use the knife to cut ⅛ inch (3 mm) deep into the outer edge (not into the top or bottom surface but into the edge) of the ring. Use the pencil ring as a guide.

6. Bend the top surface of the edge of the ring up and the bottom surface of the edge of the ring down at the pencil mark. The bends should be at about a 45° angle, as shown. Do this all the way around the edge of the ring.

CROSS SECTION OF RING

TOP

BEND UP

CUT →

← CUT

BEND DOWN

7. Toss your ring. If it curves to the left, push the bottom flap down a little more. If it curves to the right, push the upper flap up a little more. When it flies straight, you've made a cardboard version of the Aerobie.

Answers from the Past

People all over the world have been flinging flat objects as weapons and as toys for a long time.

Thousands of years ago, the aboriginal people of Australia developed the boomerang as a weapon. A boomerang employs lift. Look at one and you'll see that the top surface is slightly curved while the bottom surface is flat. Hundreds of years ago, the Sikhs of India developed the *chackrum,* which they used as a throwing weapon. The chackrum is a metal ring with a razor-sharp outer edge, and it, too, has a curved upper surface and a flat lower surface. The chackrum is the

aniel Bernoulli, a Swiss scientist born in 1700, discovered that the faster a substance such as water or air moves over an object, the lower the pressure will be on top of the object. When you throw a Frisbee, which is curved on top, the air passes over the top more quickly than under the bottom. The faster-moving air exerts less pressure on the Frisbee's upper surface than the slower-moving air does on its lower surface. Since there is more pressure from below than there is from above, the Frisbee stays up in the air (until air friction stops its forward motion). That greater upward pressure is called **lift**, and that is what keeps a Frisbee (or an airplane) in the air. An object that produces lift, such as a Frisbee or the wing of an airplane, is called an **airfoil**.

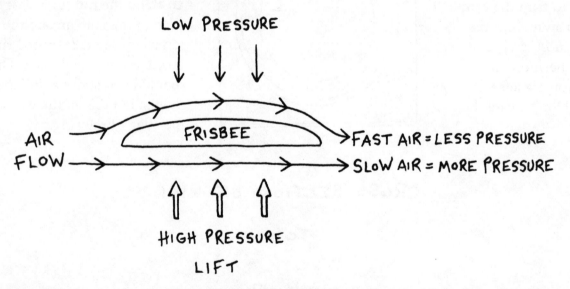

Your ring has a more complicated shape than a Frisbee. If you look at it from the side, you will see that air moving across the top has to go over the inner edges of the ring, which you bent up, while air going across the bottom does not. Because the air going over the ring has to travel a longer distance, that air travels faster than air moving under the ring, and the ring produces lift.

ancestor of the Indian *quoit,* a ring used in a game similar to horseshoes. Players tossed quoits (which have—you guessed it!—a curved upper surface), trying to get them to encircle a distant peg in the ground.

The Frisbie Pie Company in Connecticut had been baking and delivering pies for 70 years when, in the early 1940s, owner Marian Rose Frisbie made a production change. The company began to deliver the company's pies in the metal pie tins in which they were baked. The pie tins were stamped with "Frisbie Pie Company" on the bottom. College students in the company's delivery area soon discovered that they could skim the pie tins upside-down through the air, and playing catch with Frisbie pie tins became a campus game.

In 1948, Frederick Morrison, a young man who had tossed a lot of pie tins in his childhood, began experimenting with the tins to see if he could invent a toy that he could patent and sell. Plastics were a relatively new material at the time, and Morrison experimented with several different kinds. The first kind he tried was a little too brittle: his early disks tended to crack upon landing. In 1951, he used a softer plastic and developed the "Pluto Platter," which he began selling on street corners in Los Angeles. Pluto Platters sold well, and in 1955, Morrison sold his invention to a new California company called Wham-O. Wham-O renamed the toy "Frisbee" (which was a spelling mistake) after the pie tin, and has sold many millions of the toys.

> n 1968, the U.S. Navy studied Frisbees in wind tunnels. The Navy was considering whether the Frisbee shape would be a good one for airborne flares.

It was 1975 when a frustrated Alan Adler wondered whether he could redesign the Frisbee so that it would fly farther. As a sailboat designer and a lecturer in engineering at Stanford University, he knew that the Frisbee was an airfoil, but he also saw that its thick edge generated a lot of **drag** (friction with the air). Adler guessed a lighter Frisbee with a slimmer profile would travel a longer distance.

Adler first experimented with a thin disk with a slight curve. The thin disk had less drag, but it wouldn't fly straight. Next, he tried a ring shape. The ring shape was lighter, since it had less material, but it produced new problems.

A ring moving through the air is really two airfoils. The front half of the ring meets the air first, and then the back half meets the air. Adler saw that if he used a ring, he had to shape two separate airfoils: one for the outside edge of the ring and one for the inside edge. (Of course, the inside edge of the ring also formed the back part of the first airfoil and the outside edge was also the back part of the second airfoil.) Additionally, he had to deal with **backwash,** the turbulent air that flows off the end of an airfoil. The backwash from the front half of the ring created problems for the back half.

You can see why it took 10 years to design and test a flying ring that worked. Adler used a computer to sort through the combinations of angles for the leading and trailing edges of the two airfoils. He found that a few thousandths of an inch could made a big difference in the way the ring flew. The final design, called an Aerobie, is pretty good: the world's distance record for an Aerobie is over 1,200 feet (369 meters), or longer than four football fields!

INVENTOR'S CHALLENGE

Measure the length of your best throw with your flying ring. Can you make a ring of a different size or shape that will fly farther? Try different weights of cardboard or various types of plastic plates.

PART III

Inventions of Bridges and Dams

Before people learned how to build bridges, a wide, deep, swiftly flowing river could be an insurmountable obstacle. If a boat survived a crossing, the passengers would find themselves far downstream of their destination.

In many regions, the earliest bridges were made of wood. At their simplest, they were fallen trees that allowed people to cross streams or rivers up to about 50 feet (15 meters) wide. When the river was wider than a tree was tall, people learned to build **piers** (supports)—often piles of stones—in the middle of the river. Then the bridge builders could rest one fallen tree from one shore to the pier and another from the pier to the opposite shore, and people could walk across.

In tropical regions, the first bridges were made of a vine or a rope stretched between two stable points on either shore. No doubt, people first went hand-over-hand to make the crossing. Later, two ropes or vines stretched side-by-side were connected with short pieces of wood or bamboo to make a walking bridge. You will build such a bridge and see how it could have led to the invention of the suspension bridge.

In Rome, where stone was available, the arch bridge was perfected. Once Roman engineers understood how strong an arch bridge could be, they applied their knowledge to dam building. Dams built in the shape of an arch stood strong for over a thousand years.

[10] Suspension Bridge

The Problem

It is 200 B.C., and you live in a small village in China near the border of modern Tibet. Your village is surrounded by steep mountains and equally deep gorges where swift rivers run. You can't go very far from your village without having to cross one of these gorges.

You and your fellow villagers know how to weave long strips of bamboo into sturdy ropes. At several places where there are two solid trees directly opposite each other on the two sides of a gorge, you have strung a pair of ropes side-by-side across the chasm. On top of the ropes, you have laid sections of bamboo to make a walkway. Above the walkway, between the same trees, you have strung a second pair of ropes to hold on to as you cross, and in case the walkway should break.

The bridge is fine for crossing the gorge . . . unless you happen to be carrying a goat across your shoulders on your way to market. Your weight makes the bridge sharply lower wherever you stand, so from the side it looks like this [⌣] instead of like [⌣]. It's difficult to cross the bridge because you

always seem to be walking uphill and the bridge is less stable. Is there a way, you wonder, to make the bridge more stable?

Observations

When you cross with a heavy load on your back, you also notice that as your weight sinks the bridge, the hand ropes become too high. This gives you an idea . . .

MATERIALS

about forty 6-inch (15-cm)-long tongue depressors
pencil
ruler
two adult-size shoe boxes of similar size (without the tops)
adult helper
nail
two chairs of similar height with flat seats
two heavy books
7 feet (210 cm) of ¼- to ½-inch (.6- to 1.25-cm)-wide ribbon
scissors
glue
lightweight string

Experiment

1. Take one tongue depressor and use the pencil to make an X 1 inch (2.5 cm) in from each end.

2. Put one shoe box, open side down, on the table. On the bottom of the box, label one short side "top" and the other short side "bottom."

3. Measure about 1 inch (2.5 cm) from the end marked "top." Center the tongue depressor across the width of the box at that point. Make marks above each X on the tongue depressor, as shown. Measure 3 inches (7.5 cm) from the

end marked "bottom." Center the tongue depressor across the width of the box at that point. Make marks above each X on the tongue depressor.

4. Repeat Steps 2 and 3 for the second box.

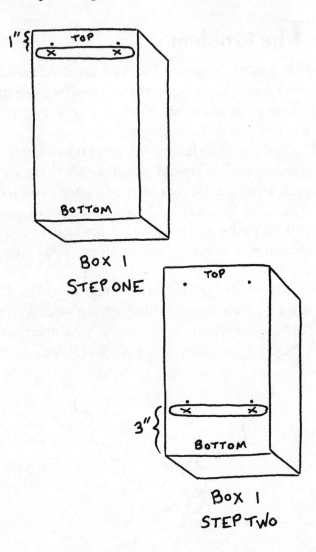

BOX 1
STEP ONE

BOX 1
STEP TWO

5. Ask an adult helper to use a nail to make holes where the marks are. The holes should be big enough for you to put the ribbon through.

6. Put the chairs facing each other and about 2 feet (60 cm) apart. Put one box upright on the front edge of one chair. The "top" end should be up and the open side of the box should face the chair back. Repeat for the other box and chair. Put a heavy book in each box to anchor it.

7. Measure and cut about 7 feet (210 cm) of ribbon. (This is your bamboo rope.) From the back of one box, push one end of the ribbon through one of the bottom holes. Push the other end of the ribbon through the other bottom hole. Stretch the ends to the holes directly opposite in the other box, as shown. Tie the ends in a knot inside the second box. Adjust the chairs so that the ribbons sag very slightly.

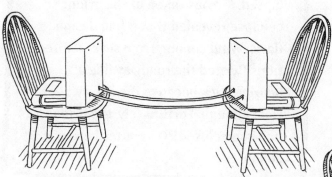

8. Put spots of glue 1 inch (2.5 cm) in from both ends of a tongue depressor. Place the tongue depressor, glue side down, across the ribbons so that the spots of glue are on the ribbons. Press in place.

9. Repeat with more tongue depressors until the ribbons are covered with tongue depressors. Leave about 1/16 inch (2 mm) of space between the tongue depressors. This is your bamboo walkway.

10. Repeat Step 7, using string instead of ribbon and using the upper holes of each box.

The string is your guide rope. Put a little pressure in the middle of the walkway and see what happens to it.

11. Measure the distance between the top and bottom holes in the boxes. Cut 12 pieces of string 2 inches (5 cm) longer than that distance.

12. Tie one end of each string to the hand rope every 4 inches (10 cm) and let it hang down.

13. Tie the other end of each string to the ribbon between the tongue depressors directly below, as shown.

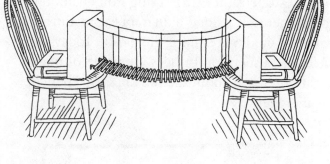

14. Put pressure on the walkway again. Notice how the hand rope tightens and resists the pressure. The tension in the hand rope prevents the walkway from sinking as far as it did before. You've made a better walkway by turning it into a suspension bridge!

Suspension bridges work because the ropes (or cables) are under tension, pulling against the towers. The towers resist the pull because they are firmly anchored to the ground (just as your towers are anchored to the chairs by books). The weight of the roadway and the traffic increases the tension on the cables. If the bridge is properly designed, the load never produces more tension than the cables can bear.

Answers from the Past

No one knows exactly who invented the first suspension bridge or how. The dangers of walking on a suspended rope walkway certainly could have inspired a thoughtful bridge builder. We do know that early suspension bridges were built out of bamboo rope about 200 B.C. in the rugged terrain of northwestern China.

Bamboo suspension bridges were common in ancient China. In A.D. 300, the Chinese built the Anlan bamboo suspension bridge across the Min River. The bridge spanned over 1,000 feet (307 meters), which is longer than three football fields. The Anlan Bridge still stands today. Its bamboo rope wasn't replaced with steel cable until 1975.

In the sixth century, the Chinese constructed the first suspension bridge using iron chain. The iron suspension bridge didn't appear in Europe or the United States until the 1700s. Today, the cables on suspension bridges are made of many steel wires (each about the thickness of a pencil) woven together.

Steel-cable suspension bridges can span longer distances than any other kind of bridge, although they are the most expensive to build. The Akashi Kaikyo Bridge (6,467 feet or 1,990 meters) in Japan and the Humber Bridge (4,624 feet or 1,423 meters) in England have the world's longest distances spanned by suspension bridges.

In 1940, the Tacoma Narrows Bridge, a suspension bridge connecting the Olympic Peninsula with the mainland in the state of Washington, was completed. It was a particularly beautiful bridge, with its slender towers and narrow roadway. Four months after the bridge opened to traffic, though, it collapsed. Movies taken of the bridge's collapse revealed that it had design flaws. Wind coming from several directions twisted the roadway like a licorice stick because the deck wasn't rigid enough. Fortunately, the bridge had been closed 20 minutes before it collapsed.

INVENTOR'S CHALLENGE

Test the strength of your suspension bridge by adding objects to the roadway. Add objects until the bridge is on the verge of collapse. Make a list of the objects. Put your suspension bridge aside.

Now, using only tongue depressors and glue (and the stacks of books as bridge anchors), build any bridge you like between the two chairs. How many of the objects that you put on your suspension bridge can your new bridge support? Can you design a bridge that holds all of these objects and more?

11 Arch Dam

The Problem

You're a senior engineer with the imperial Roman army assigned to work in Gaul (part of modern France) in A.D. 100. The town of Saint-Remy in south-eastern Gaul needs a steady supply of water for drinking and washing. The army has been ordered to build a dam on the nearby river so that water will collect behind it and become the city's reservoir.

You've seen a dam fail and it was an awful sight. (It was certainly not good for the senior engineer's career, either.) You want to make absolutely sure this dam will stand strong. How can you design a stronger dam?

Observations

Growing up in Rome, you have seen how well an arch shape supports bridges. For over 200 years, Roman engineers have been using bridges supported by arches to span valleys and rivers. You also see a number of **aqueducts** (troughs or pipes that transport water) that rest on top of arches.

MATERIALS

ruler

kitchen or laundry sink (one with a flat bottom and sides)

two sheets of poster board about 22 × 28 inches (55 × 70 cm)

pencil

scissors

modeling clay

measuring cup

Experiment

1. Measure the height and width of your sink. Cut a piece of poster board whose width and height are identical to your sink's height and width. This is your dam.

2. Put a large hunk of modeling clay on a table and roll it with the palm of your hand to form a rope about ¼ inch (60 mm) in diameter and as long as the width of your sink. Place it across the width of the bottom of the sink, about ⅔ of the way to one end, and press it down firmly. Make more clay rope and attach pieces to the side walls at the same point, as shown.

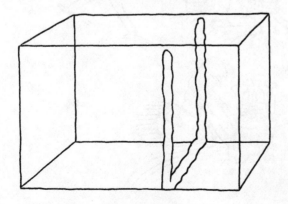

3. Place the poster board dam across the width of the sink. Sink the dam's edges firmly into the clay ropes. Press the clay tightly to the dam and to the sink to make a watertight seal. Add more clay as needed.

4. With a measuring cup, add water carefully to the bigger side of the sink, as shown. Keep track of how many cups it takes before your dam begins to leak. Keep pouring water in until your dam bursts. Make a note of how many cups it took to make the dam burst.

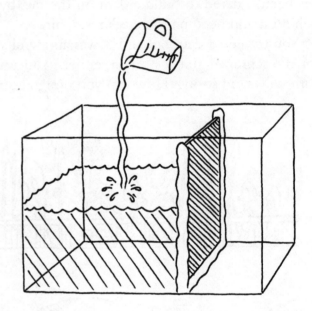

5. Remove the poster board, drain the sink, and remove the clay rope from the bottom of the sink. Leave the clay ropes on the side in place.

6. Cut a piece of poster board that is 1½ times the width of your sink. Bend the poster board so that the bend points into the bigger side of the sink. Sink the dam edges into the clay ropes on the side. Make sure the bottom of the dam rests on the bottom of the sink. Press the clay tightly to the dam and to the sink to make a watertight seal.

7. Make more clay ropes. Press them on either side of the dam at the bottom, making a watertight seal again.

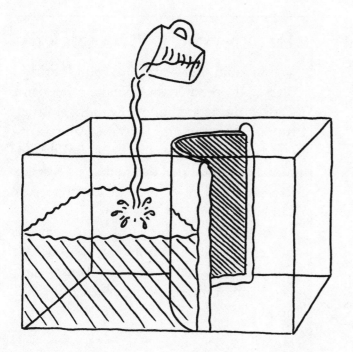

8. Repeat Step 4. Which dam held the most water?

Answers from the Past

People have been building dams for thousands of years to supply water and generate power. The oldest manmade dam that archaeologists have found is one built in Jordan in the Middle East about 3000 B.C. Around 1800 B.C., the Egyptians built a dam that operated until A.D. 1800, which means it was in use for 3,600 years!

Dams in those ancient days were **gravity dams.** In a gravity dam, the sheer weight of all the dam material—usually a combination of dirt, clay, and stones—piled in the path of a river prevents the water from following its natural course. Gravity dams go straight across a stream or river.

The Romans were great engineers. They built tunnels and aqueducts, and when they started building dams, they brought one critical invention and one superbly refined idea to their projects: concrete. The concrete they made was a mixture of sand, gravel, burnt lime (a mineral), and water. The Romans also added volcanic ash, which allowed the concrete to harden under water. By pouring wet concrete into the space between two wooden walls or *forms,* the Romans could make walls in any shape.

Concrete, the Romans discovered, is very strong under **compression** (the force that tends to squeeze matter together). It is an excellent building material for dams because dams need to stand up to the pressure of the pushing force of rivers. We still use concrete for supports for bridges and stadiums and for road surfaces, which must bear many thousands of pounds of weight. All modern dams use concrete.

The important idea that the Romans applied to dam building was the arch. The Romans had borrowed the idea from the Etruscans, who were the first to use it in about 500 B.C. in their bridges. The Romans started to build arch bridges in about 200 B.C. In about A.D. 100, Roman army engineers combined their invention of concrete and their expertise with arches to make concrete arch dams. They built the first concrete arch dam outside Saint-Remy in modern France.

Knowledge of how to build arch dams was lost after the fall of the Roman Empire in about A.D. 500. It wasn't until 1632 that an arch dam was built in Europe again. Today, many famous dams use the arch. One of the tallest is the Mauvoisin dam in Switzerland, which is 812 feet (250 meters) high, or about as tall as an 80-story building. Around the world, dams are holding back a lot of river water. If all the world's dams were torn down, sea levels would rise by 1.2 inches!

INVENTOR'S CHALLENGE

When engineers want to build bridge piers in deep water, they build a coffer dam. **Coffer dams** are hollow, cylindrical structures that are built in the water. After a coffer dam is in place, the water inside the dam can be pumped out so that a dry space is created where a stone or concrete pier can be built.

Fill a flat-bottom sink with several inches of water. Using the materials below, can you build a series of coffer dams? Using Legos or similar building blocks, can you build piers and a road surface?

Materials

    modeling clay
    Popsicle sticks
    packing tape
    turkey baster

PART IV

Inventions That Use Sound

Without air, you can't hear sounds. That's because you hear sound when an object moves and makes the air around it **vibrate** (move rapidly). These vibrations move through the air in waves. When the moving air reaches your ears, you hear sound.

Your outer ear collects the vibrations (or **sound waves**) traveling through the air and directs them to the eardrum. Your eardrum, a piece of thin tissue, vibrates, too, and moves three tiny bones—the *malleus,* the *incus,* and the *stapes*—in your inner ear. These bones move a fluid through a curvy tube in your ear called the *cochlea.* The fluid moves tiny hairs inside the cochlea, and the tiny hairs trigger nerves that lead to the brain. Your brain then interprets the nerves' signals as particular sounds.

People have been inventing devices to manipulate sound waves for many thousands of years. Various kinds of musical instruments such as flutes (wind instruments) and drums (percussion instruments) have been found around the world at sites tens of thousands of years old. Harps and other string instruments are several thousand years old.

Inventors of the modern age continue to develop musical instruments, as you will see in this section. Inventors have also learned to manipulate sound in other ways. Stethoscopes, hearing aids, and speakers are just a few of the inventions that collect or generate sound waves so that we can hear sounds more loudly, clearly, and over great distances.

12 Stethoscope

The Problem

It is 1816, and you are a French doctor named René Theophile Hyacinthe Laënnec who is about to examine a young female patient. You suspect your patient has heart disease. To diagnose her illness, you need to listen to her heart, but you're quite uncomfortable about it: The only way to hear your patient's heartbeat is to put your ear to her chest. You must listen to her heart, but how can you do it without getting so close?

Observations

Someone once pointed out to you that if you put one end of a piece of wood next to your ear and scratch the other end with a pin, you can hear the scratching sound remarkably clearly. Sounds travel well through the wood. This gives you an idea . . .

MATERIALS

24 sheets of typing, copier, or other similar paper

tape

about 12 inches (30 cm) of plastic tubing. The diameter of the tubing must be large enough so that the tubing will fit over the small ends of the funnel (available at hardware stores or stores that sell aquarium equipment).

two kitchen funnels

a friend

Experiment A

1. Put the 24 pieces of paper in a stack.

2. Roll the stack lengthwise into a tight tube. Use tape to hold the roll in place, as shown.

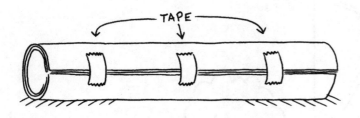

3. Place one end of the tube a little to the left of the middle of your friend's chest. Listen. Can you hear your friend's heartbeat? You've made the first *monaural* (single-ear) **stethoscope** exactly as its inventor, René Laënnec, made it!

Experiment B

1. Fit one end of the tubing over the small end of a funnel. Fit the other end of the tubing over the small end of the other funnel.

2. Tape the tubing to the funnel.

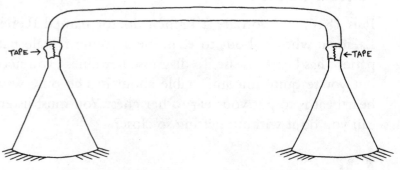

3. Put the large end of one funnel a little to the left of the middle of your friend's chest. Put the other funnel to your ear. Can you hear your friend's heartbeat? This kind of stethoscope, a monaural stethoscope with a flexible tube, was a later development.

Answers from the Past

When French physician René Laënnec faced his embarrassing problem in 1816, he recalled what he had known about the way sound travels through a solid object. Then, he picked up 24 sheets of paper and rolled them into a tight tube. He put the end of the tube to his patient's chest and listened at the other, and he was delighted to

The funnel on your friend's chest captures the sound waves generated by his or her heart and directs them in one direction: up the tube. With a stethoscope, fewer of the sound waves generated by the beating heart are lost by traveling in other directions in the air. When sound waves arrive at the other end of a stethoscope, the other funnel ensures that the sound waves are all directed to the listener's ear.

find he could hear his patient's heart quite clearly. The tube directed almost all of the sounds through the material of the tube itself and through the air inside the tube to his ear.

When you listen through a stethoscope, you hear sounds more loudly. The loudness of sounds is measured in **decibels**. (Decibels are named for Alexander Graham Bell, inventor of the telephone and other devices.) Your friend's heartbeat, heard through a stethoscope, is probably about 40 decibels. A crack of thunder is about 110 decibels. Sounds of greater than 140 decibels can damage your eardrums because the pressure of the sound waves on them is too great.

After making his paper tube, Laënnec set up a small woodworking shop in his home, and began to make what he called stethoscopes (*stetho* comes from the Greek word for "chest" and *scope* means "a device for seeing") out of hollow wooden cylinders. Using his stethoscope, Laënnec was able to refine physicians' understanding of heart and lung diseases. He published a book on his findings in 1819.

Inventors improved the monaural stethoscope by adding a flexible silk-covered coil that allowed doctors to listen in a more comfortable position. In the 1850s, inventors experimented with *binaural* (for two ears) stethoscopes. The chief advantage of the binaural stethoscope is that, in sending sound to both ears, it prevents distracting sounds from interfering with listening. Around 1910, manufacturers began to put a flexible membrane over the bell-shaped chest piece. The membrane improved the transmission of higher-pitched sounds.

INVENTOR'S CHALLENGE

Let's say you are a naturalist and you want to collect and record the sounds made by birds during the day or by insects on a summer night. You have a tape recorder and a microphone, but discover that the microphone doesn't pick up the sounds very well. Can you design a sound collector that will collect and direct the sounds to the microphone?

Experiment with a tape recorder, a microphone, a blank tape, and materials you can find around your house. What design for a sound collector produces the loudest sounds on the tape?

13 Kazoo

The Problem

You are Alabama Vest, an African American musician in Macon, Georgia, in the 1840s, and you're looking to give your music a new sound. Your parents have told you about an ancient African instrument that their grandparents heard. The instrument was made from a hollow bone or horn and had a hole in the top. The hole on the top or one of the open ends of the bone was covered with a thin, nearly transparent piece of animal tissue or a piece of the covering of a spider's egg sac. Anyone could play the instrument, which was known as a **mirliton**, because all you had to do was hum into it.

Perhaps you could revive the mirliton and bring the sound to a new audience in America. But hollow bones and spiders' egg sacs are hard to come by. What else can you use?

Observations

In the second half of the nineteenth century, everybody is using the new factory-produced tin pots, pans, plates, spoons, and other kitchen utensils. Tin is a popular material because it is cheap. It is also soft, which makes it easy to shape.

At the same time that Vest was developing a tin mirliton, Englishman Charles Clarke invented the tin whistle. Until 1843, English whistles had been made of wood. The new tin whistles (also called *pennywhistles* because they cost a penny) were an instant hit.

MATERIALS

scissors

empty toilet paper roll

scotch tape

approximately 6- × 6-inch (15- × 15-cm) piece of aluminum foil

one-hole puncher

approximately 4- × 4-inch (10- × 10-cm) piece of wax paper

rubber band

Experiment

1. Use your scissors to make a 1-inch (2.5-cm) slit into the toilet paper roll starting at one end.

2. Cross one side of the slit over the other side of the slit so that the hole at the end of the roll is narrowed. Tape the edges in place.

3. Repeat Steps 1 and 2 at the other end of the roll.

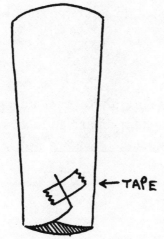

← TAPE

4. Wrap the piece of aluminum foil around the toilet paper roll and tape it in place. Trim the foil so that it does not cover the open ends of the roll.

5. Use the hole puncher to make a hole about 2 inches (5 cm) from one end of the roll. Make the hole on the straight side of the roll.

6. Place the square of wax paper over the end of the roll closest to the hole. Fold the edges of the wax paper down around the roll. Slip the rubber band over the end of the roll to hold the wax paper in place.

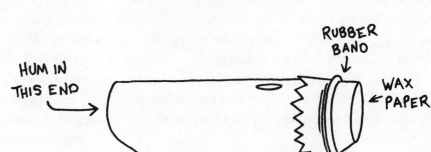

HUM IN THIS END →

RUBBER BAND ↓

WAX PAPER ←

7. Put your mouth over the open end and hum. (Just blowing won't produce a sound.) You've made a kazoo!

The body of the kazoo is a resonator—that is, a space filled with air that amplifies sound. A resonator works by bouncing the original sound back and forth among its inside surfaces so that the original sound *and* its echoes emerge. The sound waves created by your breath and voice bounce off the wax paper in your kazoo and are amplified by the resonator. Most string instruments, such as the violin and guitar, also depend on resonators.

Answers from the Past

The mirliton is an ancient African musical instrument. Mirlitons were made from all kinds of hollow materials. Archaeologists have found reed, gourd, bone, horn, and even skulls made into mirlitons. The instrument was used by witch doctors to disguise their voices so that they could present the voices of spirits and make frightening sounds. It was also used to make music.

In the 1840s, Alabama Vest designed an American version of the mirliton using tin for the body of the instrument and probably a piece of animal gut to cover the hole in the top. He took his drawings to German clockmaker Thaddeus von Clegg, who helped him produce what they called the "Down South Submarine."

The instrument was introduced to the public at the 1852 Georgia State Fair, and became popular with children and street musicians throughout the South.

No one knows what later happened to Alabama Vest and his partner. We do know that Vest and von Clegg didn't patent their invention. In 1912, a traveling salesman named Emil Sorg saw the instrument on one of his business trips and thought he could make money producing a similar product. Sorg teamed up with Michael McIntyre, a *tool and die maker* (someone who makes metal tools and machines for making metal tools) from Buffalo, New York, and set up a manufacturing plant in Buffalo for the kazoo. In 1914, they moved production to a metal manufacturing plant in Eden, New York. In 1923, McIntyre received a patent for the kazoo.

> Somehow, by the 1880s, the Deep South Submarine had also become known as a kazoo. No one knows how, but the name certainly fits!

The kazoo factory in Eden is still in operation today. Now called The Original American Kazoo Co. and owned by Brimms Inc., it is the only metal kazoo factory in the United States. The factory uses the original 1914 machines to produce over two million kazoos of all different shapes and sizes each year. It also has the world's largest kazoo (about 4 feet or 1.3 meters long) perched on its roof. If you're ever in Eden, New York, you can take a tour of the factory and visit its kazoo museum!

INVENTOR'S CHALLENGE

Can you make simple string instruments that use a resonator? Experiment with different containers to see which ones produce the loudest sounds. Does the material you use for the resonator and the strings influence the loudness? Can you make each string sound a different note?

Materials

piece of wood
small screws
plastic storage containers, shoe boxes, metal boxes
twine, fishing line, rubber bands, thin wire

14 Bottle Organ

The Problem

You are an engineer named Gary Rickert at Peterson Electro-Musical Products, Inc., in Alsip, Illinois, in early 1998. Peterson produces electronic controls for the keyboards of pipe organs, as well as tuners that help musicians **tune** (adjust the sound of the notes) their instruments. The fiftieth anniversary of the company is coming up later in the year. A big celebration is planned, and you would like to contribute to the entertainment using your professional skills. Suddenly, you have an idea . . .

Observations

Your experience at Peterson has taught you a lot about pipe organs. Pipe organs, often used in churches and orchestras to make grand-sounding music, are played with a keyboard. When an organ player strikes a key on an organ's keyboard, air blows through one of the many pipes that rise behind and above the organ's keyboard. The pipes are of all different sizes. The sound of a particular organ note depends on the length and width of the pipe through which the air blows.

When you were a kid, you drank sodas out of glass bottles. You knew that when you blew across the top of a soda bottle at just the right angle, a sound—a musical note—came out of the bottle. The note's sound depended on how much soda was left in the bottle.

MATERIALS

ruler

pen

three plastic soda straws

scissors

three empty, clean 10-oz. (296-ml) glass soda
   bottles

water

access to a piano, recorder, xylophone, or other
   musical instrument

masking tape

empty cereal box

one-hole puncher

stack of paper (any kind) about ¼ inch
   (.5 cm) tall

Experiment

1. Using your ruler, make a mark 5 inches (13 cm) from the end of your straws. (If you have straws with an accordion bend, first snip off the end of the straw with the bend.)

2. Cut the straws at the mark. Save the 5-inch (13-cm) pieces and throw away the other pieces.

3. Fill a soda bottle about half full with water.

4. Rest a straw on the rim of the bottle so that one end is about halfway across the bottle opening. Aim the straw at a slightly downward angle.

5. Blow gently through the straw. Some of the air should go down into the bottle and some should blow across the top. Adjust the angle of the straw until the bottle sounds a note.

6. Play C on the piano, recorder, xylophone, or other instrument. Does your bottle play C? If your bottle plays a note higher than C, pour some water out of the bottle. If your bottle plays a note lower than C, add some water to the bottle. When your bottle plays C, put a piece of masking tape on the bottle and write "C" on the tape.

STRAW

7. Fill another bottle with a little more water than you put in the C bottle. Tune this bottle to D and label it "D."

8. Fill another bottle with a little less water than you put in the C bottle. Tune this bottle to B and label it "B."

9. Stand the cereal box on its closed end. Measure the height of your bottles. Draw a line that is ¾ inch (2 cm) taller than the bottles' height around the outside of the box. Cut the box along the line.

10. Line up your three bottles across the front of the box. Make a small horizontal line on the cereal box over the center of each bottle and ½ inch (1.25 cm) below the top edge.

11. Remove the box. Punch holes where the marks are. The bottom of each hole should touch the mark.

12. Put the box back against the three bottles. Push a straw through one hole so that one end of it is centered over the mouth of the bottle. Rest the other end of the straw on the top of the other side of the box.

13. Repeat for the other straws.

14. Using the hole puncher, make half-hole indentations at the top edge of the box where the straws rest.

15. Adjust the straws so that when you blow through them they sound their notes. You may need to put some or all of the paper under the box to make it the right height.

16. Look at the music for "Hot Cross Buns" on page 66. Move your mouth from straw to straw to play the tune. You've made a bottle organ!

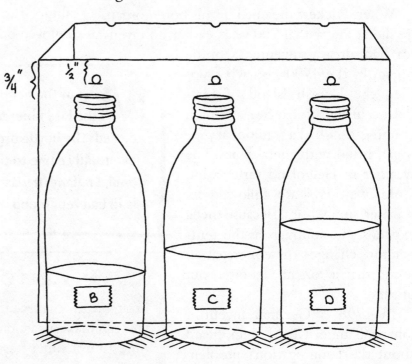

Pitch is the highness or lowness of a sound. The pitch of each of your bottles is produced when you blow into the bottle and make the air inside vibrate. The air in each bottle vibrates at a particular rate, depending on the amount of air in that bottle.

Instruments such as the flute, saxophone, and trombone have finger holes, valves, or slides that musicians use to change the length of the column of air inside their instrument as they play. When the length of the column of vibrating air changes, the pitch of the instrument changes.

Answers from the Past

Gary Rickert at Peterson Electro-Musical Products, Inc., invented a bottle organ for his company's fiftieth anniversary celebration. The organ looks like a pipe organ, except that nozzles direct air across the tops of 74 bottles partially filled with mineral oil. Rickert used his knowledge of pipe organ design and electronic tuners to build and tune his bottle organ. He used mineral oil because, unlike water, it won't evaporate and change the notes. The Peterson bottle organ can be played by pressing keys on the organ keyboard. It can also be played via a computer. The computer sends electronic signals to each nozzle to tell it when to blow air across the bottle beneath it.

The Peterson bottle organ travels to industry trade shows where it helps advertise Peterson's products. You can see photographs of the bottle organ and listen to bottle organ music by visiting www.petersontuners.com.

When Rickert dreamed up his bottle organ, he didn't know that 200 years earlier, an inventor had already invented a bottle organ. In the 1790s, on what was then the Danish island of Helgoland in the North Sea, a church congregation had a traditional pipe organ fitted with metal pipes. The weather in Helgoland varies a lot. Cold, wet days are followed by warmer, sunny ones. Because metal expands and contracts as the temperature changes, the congregation found that its organ was often out of tune.

In 1798, a German inventor, Johann Samuel Küehlewein, heard about the congregation's problem and put his creative mind to solving it. He decided to replace the metal pipes with glass bottles because temperature variations of the degree experienced on Helgoland do not affect glass. Küehlewein built an organ made of over 100 hand-blown glass bottles, some as tall as 12 inches (30 cm) and some as small as 1 inch (2.5 cm). He arranged the bottles on their sides in a rack. A **bellows** (an accordion-shaped leather pouch that pushes out air through a narrow mouth) attached to nozzles directed air over the open ends of the bottles. The bottle organ was shipped to Helgoland, where the congregation enjoyed bottle organ music for almost 100 years.

Most of the people of Helgoland left the island in the late nineteenth century and the church closed. The bottle organ was sold and sold again, and eventually came to the Merseyside Museum in Liverpool, England. It was on display for many years, but now is in bad repair and in storage.

INVENTOR'S CHALLENGE

Your breath makes air vibrate in your bottle organ, but you can make air vibrate in other ways. Can you make and tune an instrument using the following materials?

Materials

piece of wood	hammer
tacks	rubber bands

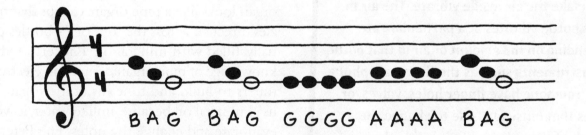

BAG BAG GGGG AAAA BAG

HOT CROSS BUNS. HOT CROSS BUNS. ONE-A-PENNY TWO-A-PENNY, HOT CROSS BUNS.

PART V

Inventions for Heating and Cooling

Heat is one of several forms of energy. When your hands are cold on a winter day, if you rub them back and forth against each other, they get warm. You have changed the energy of motion (**mechanial energy**) into **heat energy**.

When you stop rubbing your hands, they cool down. They are losing energy to the air around them. Heat energy is being **conducted** (passing by direct contact) to the air. Fortunately, your body is producing **chemical energy** by breaking down the foods that you've eaten so that your hands don't become as cold as the winter air. Energy is required to make any substance warmer or cooler than the surrounding environment.

Thousands of years ago, human beings began to invent devices to capture or produce energy so that they could heat the air and the water around them. The first heat invention was the fire pit, an arrangement of stones in a shallow hole in the ground where people laid their fires. The heated stones **radiated** (sent out) warmth into the air.

Later, people invented fireplaces, stoves, and ovens to better radiate and direct the heat of their fires. As you will see in this section, the ancient Romans invented devices that captured the sun's energy to heat their buildings and water. People have long used devices to take heat from air and water, too. They used ice cut and stored in winter to cool their homes, water, and food. You can also keep food cool even in the desert without ice or electricity. Read on in this section to find out how.

15 Solar Water Heater

The Problem

You are a manufacturer of stoves and water heaters in Baltimore, Maryland, in 1891. Your water heaters are tanks attached to the kitchen stove, which uses either gas or coal to heat both the food on the stove and the water in the tank. Both fuels have significant drawbacks. Gas, made by burning coal in an airless environment, is expensive. It also produces an oily residue that settles from the air onto furniture and walls. Heating with coal is even messier. Burning coal produces smoke and ashes, as well as an awful smell.

You'd like to invent a better method for heating water, especially in the summer. It's torture to be indoors on a blistering summer day in Baltimore when the stove is going full blast to heat water.

Observations

In the 1800s, some Americans heat water by taking a metal tub, painting it black, filling it with water, and putting it in the sun. On a warm, sunny day, sunlight can heat the cold water by afternoon. The problem is there is no hot water in the morning, and when the sun goes down, the hot water cools off quickly. In the winter in many parts of the country, this hot water heater doesn't work at all because the air is too cold.

MATERIALS

black electrical tape

empty soda can

water

scissors

rectangular plastic deli container that is deep enough to hold the soda can when the can is on its side. The container must have a clear upper half.

black felt (about the size of your deli container)

glue

candy or meat thermometer (Do not use a fever thermometer: the water in your solar water heater will exceed the thermometer's limit.)

Experiment

1. Wrap black electrical tape around the outside of the soda can so that the can is entirely black.

2. Fill the can with cold water.

3. Cut the piece of black felt to fit the bottom of the deli container. Glue it in place. Let the glue dry.

4. Prop up the deli container against a wall. Place the can against the felt and tape it in place, as shown. Close the lid of the plastic container. This is your solar water heater.

5. With your scissors, make a hole in the plastic above the opening in the can. Place the candy or meat thermometer through the hole and into the can, as shown.

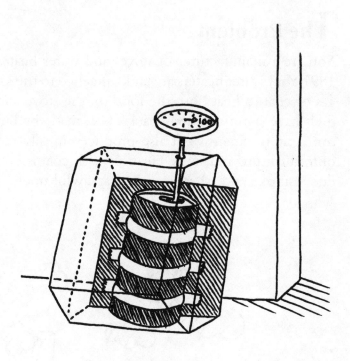

6. Prop up your water heater in the sun so that it catches the full sun. You can do this inside or outside when the temperature is above 65°F (18°C). Measure the temperature of the water every hour. When the water temperature is 100°F (38°C), your bath water is ready!

The sun emits **photons**, which are tiny bits of energy. We perceive the photons as light and heat. Black objects absorb photons and white objects reflect them. Try wearing a black T-shirt outside on a hot, sunny day. When you start to feel hot, switch to a white T-shirt. How does it feel?

The clear plastic of your solar water heater allows light to pass to the black can. The light energy is absorbed by the can, heating it and the water inside. The air in the water heater also is heated directly by photons and by heat energy **radiated** (sent out) from the black felt and black can. The plastic cover and the warmed air under it insulate the can from the cooler air outside the heater, so the water doesn't lose heat.

Answers from the Past

The ancient Romans went to large public baths to wash themselves, play games, and socialize. For many years, they heated the water in the baths with wood-burning fires. Eventually, they had an energy crisis: they had cut down most of the trees within easy range of Rome.

The Romans decided to conserve their remaining forests by using **solar** (which comes from the Latin word *solaris,* meaning "sun") energy to heat the baths. They installed glass in the south-facing walls of the bathhouses, which were exposed to the sun for the longest period of time. The windows passed the heat energy of the sun into the water and air of the baths, while slowing the escape of the heated air back to the outside air.

People bathed regularly in Rome, thanks to the heated public baths, but the practice, and the technique of using the sun to heat water, died out in Europe after the fall of the Roman Empire in about A.D. 500. Hardly anyone bathed regularly in Europe or America again until the 1800s. Perfumes became popular: they covered up the odor of unwashed bodies.

Clarence Kemp, a manufacturer of water heaters, began experimenting with solar water heaters in the 1880s, and he patented his product, the Climax Solar-Water Heater, in 1891. Each unit contained four long, cylindrical water tanks made of heavy galvanized iron painted black. They lay next to each other in a pine box lined with black felt paper and covered by a sheet of glass. The box was usually installed on a sloped roof to catch the sun's rays, and was connected to the bathroom and kitchen below by pipes. To get solar-heated water, you simply turned the faucet.

One good reason for skipping baths was that heating bath water was tedious and expensive. Here's one nineteenth-century rural American's description of what it took to take a bath:

"You took just one bath a week, a Saturday night deal, because it was such hard work to heat the water on the stove. You put the water in pots, pails, anything which would hold water and you could lift. It took a while for those old stoves to get going because the heat first had to penetrate through the heavy metal."

The hot water was poured into a tin tub, and then everyone in the family, one after another, took a bath. By the time the last person got in, the water was not very hot or clean!

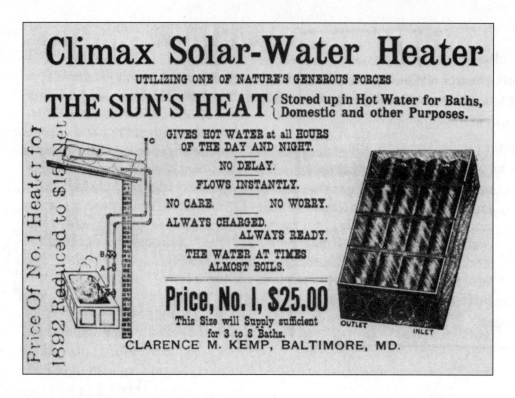

Over the years, inventors made many improvements to Kemp's original design. The large tanks became coiled copper pipes that heated the smaller amount of water inside them more quickly. The glass-covered box (the "collector box") became shallower and much larger, so more pipe was exposed to the sun. The copper pipes ran the heated water to a tank inside the house where the water wouldn't be cooled at night by falling temperatures. Thick insulation around the tank reduced heat loss, by 1909, to less than 1° per hour.

Kemp's smallest solar water heater sold for $15 in 1892 and saved a family $10 or more each year on coal or gas. The water heaters sold well, especially in southern California, where the climate is warm all year and the heaters could be used year-round. In northern states, the water heaters could only provide hot water from early April through October, so they were not as popular.

Today, over 1.5 million American families use solar-heated water. Those people who use solar energy protect the environment from the pollution that results from burning fossil fuels (oil, gas, and coal). They also reduce their monthly energy bills because, of course, sunlight is free.

However, there are drawbacks to heating water with solar energy. In many places in the United States, there are periods of time when it is either too cool or too cloudy to rely on solar energy. Trees may also block the sunlight. In addition, the initial cost of installing a solar water heater can be high, even though continuing costs are low. Especially for people who already have one kind of water heater, it is expensive to replace the existing system with a new solar system.

INVENTOR'S CHALLENGE

Figure out how long it takes your heater to heat water to a particular temperature. Can you invent a more efficient water heater? How fast can you heat water to bath temperature? Use some of the following materials or add your own.

Materials

aluminum foil
additional deli lids
different-shaped containers for the water
black plastic bag
plastic tubing

16 Desert Refrigerator

The Problem

It is 1995 and you are a 36-year-old teacher in Nigeria, a country on the west coast of Africa. In some of the poor rural villages in the northern part of Nigeria where you have lived and worked, there is no electricity. Even in the few towns that have electricity, the power often goes off for days or weeks at a time. This means that refrigeration is nearly nonexistent.

Much of northern Nigeria is arid and dry, and most of the people who live there are poor farmers. In the constant heat and without refrigeration, the farmers' produce gets moldy and spoils within a couple of days. The little extra fruit and

VEGETABLES

vegetables that the farmers grow to sell for cash must be sold quickly before they rot. Unfortunately, that means that the daughters of a household, instead of going to school, are sent to town to sell the produce in the streets.

You are among a small minority of Nigerian adults with a college education. You are determined to improve the lives of your fellow Nigerians, especially the girls who are missing an education. What can you do?

Observations

You grew up in northern Nigeria in a family of potters. In northern Nigeria, clay pots have been used for thousands of years as cooking and storage vessels and even as coffins. Although pottery containers are rapidly being replaced by aluminum containers, you are very familiar with pottery. In particular, you remember how wonderfully cool a damp clay pot is before it's **fired** (baked) in a kiln.

MATERIALS

three *unglazed* flowerpots: two pots about
  4 inches (10 cm) in diameter at the top and
  one pot about 6 inches (15 cm) in diameter
  at the top

tape

sand

water

two pieces of fresh fruit or vegetable (or bread,
  preferably without preservatives)

two pieces of cloth each about
  8 × 8 inches (20 × 20 cm)

Experiment

1. If your flowerpots have a hole in the bottom, put a piece of tape over the holes.

2. Pour enough sand into the bottom of the large pot so that when a smaller pot is placed on the sand,

the rims of the two pots are level. Center one of the smaller pots in the larger one. Pour sand into the space between the two pots so that the space is filled nearly to the rims of the pots. Pour water on the sand until the sand is thoroughly wet. This is your desert refrigerator.

3. Put a piece of fruit or bread in the desert refrigerator. Put a similar piece in the remaining small pot.

4. Wet one piece of cloth and then wring it out so that it is damp but not dripping. Cover the desert refrigerator with the damp cloth. Put the dry piece of cloth over the single pot, as shown.

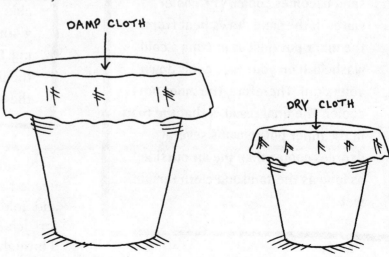

5. Put the desert refrigerator and the single pot in a warm, dry place but not in direct sunlight. Keep the sand in the desert refrigerator wet. Keep the cloth on the desert refrigerator damp, too.

6. Look at the food in both pots every day. How long does the desert refrigerator keep the food fresh? How about the food in the single pot?

It is important that the sand remain wet in your desert refrigerator and that you use the refrigerator when the air is warm and dry. Here's why. The sand holds water. The water slowly seeps through the wall of the larger pot, where it turns into water vapor and evaporates when it meets dry, circulating air. Water vapor is water whose molecules are moving faster and farther apart than water. In order for the water vapor molecules to move faster, they must gain energy. That energy comes from the water they leave behind. Because heat is a form of energy and energy leaves the water, the water in the sand becomes cooler. The cooler water in the sand draws heat from the inner pot (just as putting a cold washcloth on your face cools down your skin). Therefore, the inner pot is cooler. The final result is that the food in the inner pot remains several degrees cooler than the air outside, as long as the sand and cloth remain wet.

Answers from the Past

Food spoils when bacteria and fungi grow on it and eat it. Tens of thousands of years ago, human beings who lived in cold climates discovered that if they let an animal carcass freeze, it would not rot. That's because bacteria and fungi don't thrive (although they may survive) at temperatures below freezing. In Russia, near the town of Mezhirich, archaeologists have discovered refrigeration pits that people cut into the **permafrost** (land that is frozen year-round) about 15,000 years ago.

People around the world have taken advantage of the fact that ice preserves food. About 1000 B.C., the Chinese began to cut and store ice to use in the summer. In 500 B.C., the Egyptians made ice by leaving water in earthenware pots outside on a cold night. Around 50 B.C., the emperor of Rome cooled his wines with snow brought down from the mountains by his slaves.

Harvesting ice and shipping it to warm climates became a big business in New England in the mid-nineteenth century. Frederic Tudor of Boston (known as the Ice King) and his partner, Nathaniel Wyeth, figured out how to efficiently cut ice from frozen ponds, load it onto sailing ships, and pack it in sawdust. They were able to insulate ice so well that it survived a 4-month trip to India with minimal melting. By 1856, over 125,000 tons of ice left the port of Boston for destinations around the world.

Numerous inventors realized that people needed a machine that could reliably create ice and cold air so that they wouldn't have to wait for ice shipments from northern climates. Throughout the nineteenth century, inventors developed refrigerators that used the compression of various gases to cool. Electric refrigerators became popular after World War I.

In northern Nigeria and many other poor, desert-like areas, neither importing ice nor freezing water with expensive electricity and gases is an option. Until Mohammed Bah Abba invented the desert refrigerator, people in these areas were resigned to the rapid spoilage of fresh foods. In 1995, Abba combined his practical knowledge of pottery and his knowledge of basic **thermodynamics** (the science of the relationship between heat, energy, and work) to invent a refrigerator that is inexpensive to make and costs nothing to run.

Using formerly unemployed workers as well as skilled potters, Abba has produced about 12,000 desert refrigerators and has distributed them for free. He finds that eggplants stay fresh in the refrigerators for 27 days instead of 3 days, and that tomatoes and peppers last for 3 weeks.

Using desert refrigerators, farmers can hold their produce instead of rushing to sell it. They can get better prices, and their daughters are now free to attend school. Thanks to Abba's invention, the number of girls in elementary schools in the Jigawa region of Nigeria is rising. Abba estimates that about three-quarters of the rural families in the Jigawa region are using desert refrigerators. He hopes to make his invention available throughout northern Nigeria and elsewhere around the world.

INVENTOR'S CHALLENGE

It seems impossible that a shipful of ice blocks cut from frozen ponds could last on a 4-month voyage to the hot climate of southern India. Frederic Tudor did years of experiments to find out how to pack ice in order to preserve it so well.

Consider plastic containers to be shipping containers and find the best materials to insulate (reduce the transfer of heat from) a shipment of ice.

Materials

- ice cubes
- identical plastic containers
- insulating materials (try bubble wrap, newspaper, towels, sand, dirt, and other materials)
- kitchen scale

CLUE

Drain the water from the plastic containers and use a kitchen scale to measure which materials are doing the best job of insulating the ice cubes.

PART VI

Miscellaneous Inventions

Some inventions come about because one inspired person notices a phenomenon that no one else had looked at in quite the same way before. The ancient Egyptian water clock and the ancient Greek scytale (a ciphering device), which you will make in this section, probably were such inventions. Other inventions in this section—such as the portable solar still and the pendulum seismograph—pushed existing devices in a new direction.

As different as these inventions are, the people who invented them had a common trait. They looked at the world with fresh eyes and open minds. Have you ever stretched out on your back, looked at the ceiling, and imagined it as the floor? Try it, and see what it feels like to look at the world with fresh eyes!

[17] Water Clock

Problem

You are a priest at a sun temple in Egypt in 1500 B.C. You and your fellow priests don't live in the temple, but one of you must be there at all times, day and night. You divide the night shift evenly among yourselves, and use the movement of the stars as they pass in the night sky to gauge when a third of the night has gone. But it's hard to tell time precisely by the stars, and it seems to you that you are getting more than your fair share of the night-watch duty. How can you divide the night hours accurately?

About 3500 B.C., Egyptians began building **obelisks** (tall, slender pillars) at the entrance to temples dedicated to the sun. They put markers on the ground to the east and west of the obelisk. As the sun moved across the sky, the shadow cast by the obelisk shrank in the morning (until at noon there was no shadow at all) and grew in the afternoon. The shadow falling on the markers indicated the hour of the day.

Of course, the obelisks were of no help at night. Even during the day, they weren't much help in measuring small increments of time. There was another problem, too, with obelisks as clocks. The winter "hours" they told were shorter than their summer "hours."

How could that be? The period of daylight in winter is shorter than it is in summer. Therefore, the obelisk's shadow moves more quickly from the first marker to the last in the winter than it does in the summer. Since the obelisk divided whatever daylight there was—regardless of the season—into 12 equal pieces, a winter "hour" was shorter than a summer "hour."

Observations

You use a leather bucket to carry water from the river to the temple to perform a cleansing ritual. Back at the temple, you loop the handle of the bucket on a peg on the wall while you make your preparations. One day, when you go to reach for the bucket, you realize it's sprung a tiny leak. Some of the water has run out.

Buckets are scarce, so you keep on using your leaky one. Every day, from the time you start your preparations to the time you reach for the bucket, you notice that exactly the same amount of water has run out. The water dripping steadily out of the bucket makes you think . . .

MATERIALS
empty 1-liter plastic soda bottle
ruler
scissors
water
masking tape
pen
a few large Styrofoam cups
watch or clock with a second hand
pitcher

Experiment

1. Measure down about 3 inches (7.5 cm) from the top of the bottle. Cut off the top of the bottle.

2. Tape a piece of masking tape along the side of the bottle.

3. Pour just enough water into the bottle so that the water level is above the curved part of the bottom of the bottle. Make a mark on the masking tape at the water level.

4. Use your pen to put a small hole in the bottom of the cup. Put the cup into the open top of the bottle. The top of the cup should rest on the rim of the bottle. (If it doesn't, you need a larger cup.)

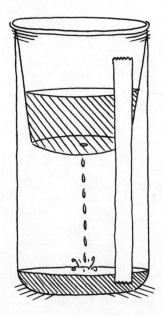

5. Pour water from a pitcher into the cup until the cup is half full. Start timing with your watch. At regular intervals (every 30 seconds, for example), mark the water level in the bottle on the masking tape. (You may need to make the hole in the bottom of the cup larger if your marks are too close together to see well.) Keep adding water to the cup so that the cup remains about half full. Number your marks from bottom to top.

6. Are the marks on the masking tape evenly spaced? Can you tell how much time has passed by looking at the marks? You've made an ancient Egyptian water clock!

7. Make different-size holes in other Styrofoam cups. Can you make a clock that measures minutes accurately? How about a clock that measures hours?

Answers from the Past

No one knows who in Egypt invented the water clock or what inspired that person, but a priest could well have been the inventor. Priests were educated and would have had a need for telling time in their rituals. Priests were responsible for the obelisk shadow clocks (which were usually part of temples), so they would have been familiar with time-keeping.

One of the world's oldest remaining water clocks was discovered in an Egyptian tomb built in 1500 B.C. The Egyptian water clocks were made of stone or pottery bowls. The markings for the hours were made on the inside of the bowl that held the water. When scientists tested these ancient clocks, they found that they were quite accurate.

The ancient Greeks refined the water clock around 400 B.C. and called it a **clepsydra,** which means "water thief."

Some of the Greek clepsydras were very complex. In one, water dripped steadily into a container that had a float in it. As the float rose, it lifted a stick that turned a dial, which indicated the time.

It was not easy to keep a water clock accurate. Over time, the flowing water could make the hole in the clepsydra's bowl wider, speeding up time; or grit could get in the hole, slowing down the clock. It was also hard to keep the flow of water to the clock constant. Of course, no two water clocks kept time in the same way, since no two bowls were identical.

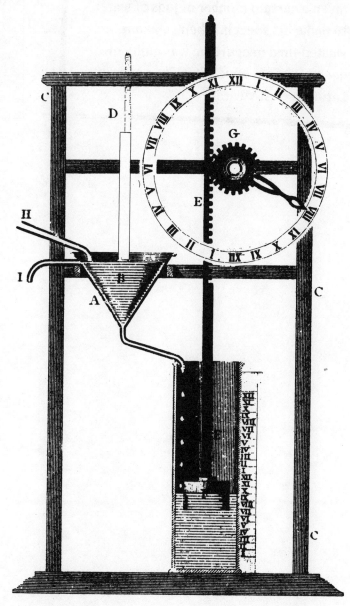

The ancient Greeks and Romans used the water clock as a timer more often than they did as a means of telling the current time. In the Roman courts of law, a water clock was used to determine the length of a trial. If the case was a minor one, a small amount of water was poured into the water clock. If the case was an important one, a large amount of water was added. Speeches by the accuser, the accused, and the judge were measured by a water clock, too. Each speaker was given a certain number of jugs of water to make his speech. When someone wasted time in court, he was guilty of *aquam perdere*, which literally means in Latin "to waste water."

INVENTOR'S CHALLENGE

You may have noticed in your experiments that the rate at which water drips out of the cup depends on how full the cup is. When the cup is full, the weight of the water quickly forces drops out of the hole. When the cup is nearly empty, there isn't much weight to force water out of the hole, so the dripping is slow. As the cup empties, the water pressure decreases, and the clock slows down.

The ancient Egyptians, Greeks, and Romans solved the problem of changing **water pressure** (the force of water). Can you invent a water clock that solves the water pressure problem? Make a water clock that keeps accurate time no matter how much water is in it.

18 Scytale

The Problem

It is about 422 B.C., and you are a general in the army of Sparta, a city-state in ancient Greece. You are preparing to send new written orders to your captain outside of Athens via a messenger. What if the messenger is captured by the Athenians? If the enemy reads these orders, it will be disastrous for your troops. You wish you could send a message that the Athenians can't read, but if the enemy can't read it, how will your captain be able to?

Observations

The long *hilt* (the handle) of your favorite iron sword is covered in a length of soft leather wrapped in a spiral. The leather has a large stain on it. One day, the leather strip comes unwound. When you stretch out the strip, you notice that sections of the stain appear periodically on the strip. When you rewrap your sword hilt, you see something interesting: the stain is pieced together exactly as it was before you unwound the strip. You wrap and unwrap the leather several times, and discover that the bits of stain on the strip always join to become the familiar, solid stain on your sword's hilt. This makes you think . . .

MATERIALS

scissors

sheet of typing, copier, or other plain white paper

two pieces of 1-inch (2.5-cm)-diameter wooden dowel, each about 6 inches (15 cm) long

tape

pen or pencil

friend

Experiment

1. Cut a ½-inch (1.25-cm) strip from the long edge of the paper. Start to spiral the paper around one dowel so that the edges touch but don't overlap, as shown. Put a small piece of tape at the beginning of the paper strip to hold it in place. After you have finished the spiral, put another small piece of tape at the end to hold the end in place.

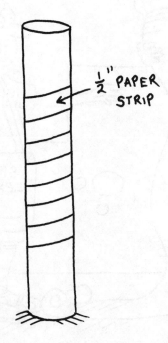

½" PAPER STRIP

2. Write a message on the paper by writing your letters in a column down the handle, as shown. Make sure that one letter is in each row of the column. When you get to the bottom of the paper, continue your message at the top of the next column. Fill up the paper in this way.

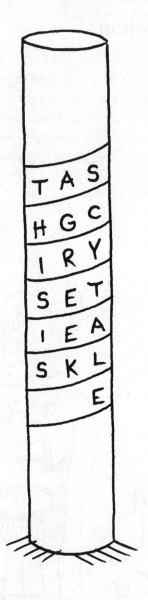

3. Take off the pieces of tape and unwrap the strip of paper (it should be a meaningless jumble of letters). Give the strip and the other piece of dowel to a friend. Show her or him how to wind the paper around the other dowel. Can your friend read the message? You've made an ancient Greek **scytale** (pronounced "sigh-tale")!

Answers from the Past

Military commanders have had to figure out how to get messages to and from headquarters for thousands of years. Early on, commanders and their captains established code words and phrases to convey secret meanings, such as "three black birds sing in the cypress" to mean "send three hundred troops to attack the city." Such a system, however, is not very flexible. What if the commander wants to say, "I've learned that the gatekeeper at the northeast gate can be bribed for 17 pieces of silver?" Also, what happens if the captain or the commander is killed? Headquarters and the troops could no longer communicate in secret.

The early scytales were wooden batons around which a strip of leather or parchment was wound. The sender wrote a message in columns, unwound the strip, and then sent the seemingly meaningless strip by messenger. The receiver wound the strip around an identical scytale and decoded the message.

We don't know who in ancient Sparta invented the scytale or exactly when it was invented. We can guess that a Spartan military officer had the idea. That's because only officers were taught to read; ordinary soldiers received only physical and military education.

We do know that a Spartan commander, Lysander, used a scytale in 404 B.C. At that time, Sparta and Athens had been fighting the Peloponnesian War for 30 years with neither side achieving decisive victory. The turning point of the war finally came when Persia entered the war on the side of Sparta. The Persians contributed money and ships to the cause. They also stationed troops near Sparta to protect the home front and allow more Spartan troops to attack the Athenians.

One day, a messenger arrived on the battlefield asking for the Spartan commander, Lysander. "What do you have for me?" Lysander asked. "I don't know. I was simply told to find you," said the messenger. Lysander then saw the man was wearing a leather belt. Branded into the belt was a series of random letters. Lysander took the belt, wrapped it around his scytale, and the random letters formed themselves into a message. The message was from home: a Persian commander in Sparta was planning to seize Sparta for himself. With that information, Lysander set off with this troops and got rid of the traitor. With the alliance intact, the Spartans vanquished the Athenians in 404 B.C.

The ancient Greek historian, Herodotus, wrote about another method of sending a secret message. The governor of the Greek city-state Miletus, Histaiaeus, was plotting against the Persian ruler, Darius. He wanted to send a message to a man named Aristagoras to join his rebellion. He selected a messenger, shaved the man's head, tattooed the message on his scalp, and when the messenger's hair had grown back, sent him off across the Persian lines. When the messenger found Aristagoras, he simply asked him to shave his head. Aristagoras joined the rebellion.

The secret message system that the Spartans developed is called a **transposition cipher.** (Codes and ciphers are similar. In **codes,** whole words are replaced; in ciphers, letters are replaced.) In a transposition cipher, the letters of a message are rearranged. For this message to make sense, you need to have a key. Consider this message: clognosmindwearatohzipsameetsostargle. What does it mean? Write down the first letter and then every other letter and see what the result is. The key to this transposition is "read every other letter, starting with the first one."

Another type of cipher is called a **substitution cipher.** Every letter is substituted with another letter. Julius Caesar, a Roman emperor born in 100 B.C., used a code in which every letter in a message was replaced by the letter three places ahead of it in the alphabet. So, *a* became *d, b* became *e, c* became *f,* and so forth. Caesar used a very simple substitution code, but these codes can be very complex. Today, computers use elaborate mathematical formulas to generate substitution codes.

INVENTOR'S CHALLENGE

Some **cryptographers** (people who make codes and ciphers) use a substitution cipher *and* a transposition cipher. To further foil the enemy, cryptographers may also use a rule for constantly changing the code.

Construct a cipher that uses substitution, transposition, and a rule for changing the cipher every day. Give a friend the cipher and exchange secret messages.

[19] Gimbal

The Problem

You are a Chinese nobleman in 200 B.C. who has just woken up with your bed on fire! You manage to put out the fire, but you can't go back to sleep. Instead, you start thinking. It is the fashion in your time—and a very pleasant fashion—to burn perfumed oil in a lamp in the bedroom. The lamps give off a beautiful scent, but, as you have just discovered, they tip easily. Among the blankets, pillows, and cloth wall hangings, they are a fire hazard. You'd like to continue using these special lamps, but not at the cost of your life. What can you do to make them safer?

Observations

You have watched farmers carrying water to their fields in buckets hung over the ends of a yoke (a piece of wood that rests on the shoulders behind the neck). The farmers rarely spill any water, even when they go uphill. The trick, you can see, is that the buckets can turn or **pivot** freely on the ends of a tilting yoke.

MATERIALS

scissors

poster board

tape

aluminum foil

paper-coated wire ties of the kind used to close plastic bags

straight pin

deep mixing bowl (with a diameter of roughly 8 inches [20 cm])

Experiment

1. Cut a 2-inch (5-cm)-diameter circle out of the poster board. Cut a slit from the side to the center. Overlap the edges to form a cone. Use tape to secure the edges of the cone. This is your perfume lamp. Line it with a little aluminum foil.

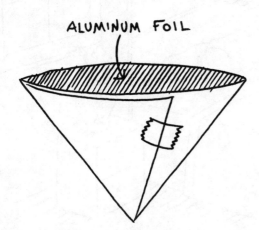

ALUMINUM FOIL

2. Cut six pieces of paper-coated wire tie, each about 1 inch (2.5 cm) long. Strip off about ⅓ inch (1 cm) of paper from each end, leaving a piece in the middle still covered with paper.

3. Cut a strip of poster board about ½ inch (1.25 cm) wide and 7 inches (17.5 cm) long. Bend the strip to form a circle and tape the ends together.

4. Poke the end of a wire tie piece through your lamp near the rim. (You may want to use a straight pin to start a hole.) Bend down the stripped end to keep the tie from falling out. Repeat on the opposite side of the lamp. Poke the other end of each tie through opposite sides of the circle. Bend their ends down, too. When you pick up the circle, the lamp should be suspended by the ties inside the circle, as shown.

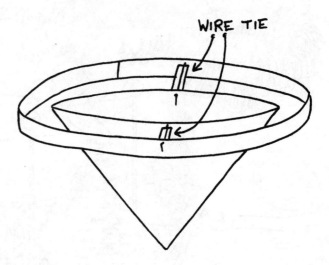

WIRE TIE

5. Put a little water in your lamp. Hold the edge of the circle in your hands and experiment with tilting it. Did you notice that when you hold it so that each hand is near a tie and you tilt the ring toward you, the lamp stays upright and no water spills? What happens if you turn the circle a quarter turn and tilt it toward you? (You can clean up the spilled water now!)

In Step 5, when you turned the circle around the axis (a line about which an object—like the earth—turns) provided by the two ties, the energy you are supplying goes into turning the circle, not the lamp. After you shifted the circle a quarter turn, your energy went into turning the circle, the axis, and the lamp. The lamp did not have a pivot on which to turn in this direction.

6. Cut a strip of poster board about 10 inches (25 cm) long. Bend it into a circle and tape the ends together.

7. Using the same procedure as in Step 4, attach the second circle to the first circle. It is important to position this set of ties in a specific place. Look at the lamp and think of the first ties as being at 9 o'clock and 3 o'clock. Attach the second set of ties at 12 o'clock and 6 o'clock.

8. Strip the paper off of one end of two uncut ties. Poke the stripped end of one of these ties about halfway between 12 o'clock and 3 o'clock. Poke the stripped end of the second tie into the outer circle about halfway between 6 o'clock and 9 o'clock. Then tape the other

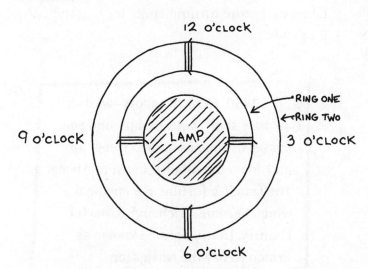

ends of both ties onto the rim of the mixing bowl, so that the nest of circles is centered within the rim.

9. Put a little water in the lamp. Now experiment by turning the mixing bowl in all directions. No matter which way you turn the bowl—even upside down—your lamp should stay level! You've made a model of an ancient Chinese perfume burner. We call it a gimbal and still use it today.

Don't try to burn oil or anything else in this lamp. It's just a model!

You will have to experiment with the measurements for the ties and paper strips. The measurements that will work for your gimbal depend on exactly how much you overlap the strips' ends and exactly how long the paper-covered sections of the wire ties are. The object is for all the circles and the lamp to turn freely.

How does a gimbal work? When the lamp was attached to only one circle, it rotated around only one axis. It spilled when it was rotated in another dimension.

We live in three-dimensional space. Once you added the other circle with a different axis and the bowl with an axis oriented in a third direction, the gimbal could turn in all three dimensions. No matter in which direction you apply energy, one of the circles turns on its axis and takes up the energy, leaving the lamp still.

Answers from the Past

A Chinese poet in about 140 B.C. first mentioned a gimbal, which he called "the metal rings containing the burning perfume." The inventor of this convenient device that could revolve in all three dimensions was said to be a man named Fang Feng. The first use of the gimbal was indeed to protect the bedclothes from catching fire.

Gimbal is an English word that originally meant "joint," "link," or "ring." You can see why this collection of rings came to be known as a gimbal.

In the following centuries, the Chinese put the gimbal to work in many other devices. In A.D. 692, the Chinese empress Wu Hou was presented with "wooden warming-stoves, which, though rolled over and over with their iron cups filled with glowing fuel, could never be upset." Later, the Chinese used gimbals to hold lamps inside spherical paper lanterns. Then people rolled the lanterns down the streets to light their way as they walked!

In the early 1400s, Prince Henry of Portugal dreamed of making his country wealthy with the gold and jewels that overland travelers brought from Africa. Traveling by land to and from Africa, however, was slow and dangerous. Prince Henry believed that a better way to get to Africa was by sailing down the Atlantic Ocean.

At the time, people were terrified of sailing the Atlantic. Out of sight of land, it was easy to lose one's location. Compasses were helpful, but only in relatively calm seas. When a compass doesn't lie flat and still, its needle can't swing freely. In 1419, Prince Henry built a school for mariners at the port of Sagres so that they could improve their skills and develop new technology. Henry's sailors learned to use the gimbal, which had arrived in Europe from China, to hold magnetic compasses. With a gimbal, the energy of the waves and wind that make a ship rock is taken up by the turning rings, leaving the compass still.

By 1450, Henry's sailors—with their new skills, better maps, and compasses in gimbals—sailed freely up and down the Atlantic coast to Africa. They made a fortune for Portugal, which became a rich and powerful country. Henry became known as Prince Henry the Navigator.

In the 1850s, Jean-Bernard-Leon Foucault, a French scientist, used the principles of the gimbal to make a gyroscope. A **gyroscope** is a gimbal that has a spinning wheel in the middle instead of a stationary lamp or a compass. Once that wheel has been set in motion, it stays pointed in the same direction and at the same angle to earth no matter how the frame of circles around it is moved. Aircraft and spacecraft use gyroscopes to keep on course through three dimensions.

INVENTOR'S CHALLENGE

Can you convert your gimbal into a gyroscope? Try various materials to make a lightweight wheel that you can set spinning in place of the lamp in the center of the gimbal.

20 Pendulum Seismograph

The Problem

You are an Italian clock maker named Domemico Salsano in Naples, Italy, in 1783. A series of tremendous earthquakes has recently rocked Calabria, a region about 200 miles away. The quakes produced **fissures** (holes) that swallowed whole houses, trees, animals, and human beings. You would like to know more about these destructive events. You wonder whether you can build a device that will measure and record earthquakes.

Observations

As a clock maker, you frequently work with **pendulums**. (A pendulum is the long, swinging stick with a weight at the end that regulates a clock's speed.) You know that when you move a clock case, the clock's pendulum remains still even as you tilt and shift the case. This makes you think . . .

> n 1583, Galileo demonstrated that when a pendulum of a particular length swings, each swing takes place in the same amount of time. A pendulum of a particular length will take a particular period of time (the **frequency**) to swing one way and return. It doesn't matter how wide the arc of the pendulum's swing is or how heavy the pendulum is—the pendulum will always take the same amount of time to complete its swing.

MATERIALS

stack of about eight heavy books

ruler with holes punched to fit in a binder

another ruler (any kind)

string

fine-point felt-tip pen

three washers with a hole large enough so that they will fit over the barrel of the pen

tape

adding machine paper or any other long, narrow strip of paper

two helpers

Experiment

1. Stack the books on a table. Slide the first ruler between the second and third books from the top in the stack. Slide about 4 inches (10 cm) of the ruler between the books.

2. Measure the distance from the end of the ruler to the tabletop. Cut a piece of string about 3 inches (7.5 cm) longer.

3. Put one end of the string through the hole at the end of the horizontal ruler. Tie—but don't knot—the string around the ruler.

4. Hold the other end of the string against and parallel to the pen. Tape the string to the pen along its length, as shown.

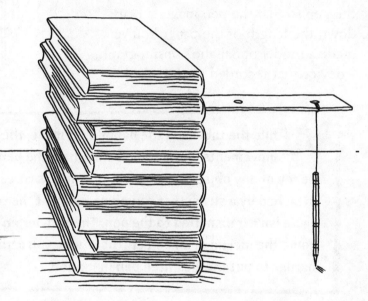

5. Slip the washers over the end of the pen. Bunch them together near the pen point. Tape the washers together and to the pen.

6. Put the strip of paper on the table so that one end is centered directly under the pen and the rest of the strip is lined up parallel to the ruler. The tip of the pen should lightly

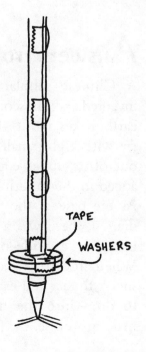

TAPE

WASHERS

touch the paper. (Untie the string where you tied it onto the ruler, and shorten or lengthen the string, if you need to. Tie it back on tightly when you're done.)

7. Ask your helpers to stand on either side of the table. They should be on the sides of the table that are parallel to the ruler. Ask them to jiggle the table, steadily but gently, between them for about 15 seconds. (Your friends are simulating an earthquake.) While they are doing this, pull the paper steadily under the pen so that the pen makes a mark down the length of the paper. You've made a model of Salsano's seismograph, a device that recorded earthquakes!

While the table and the paper on it move, the pendulum remains still and records the movements of the table beneath it. The pendulum has inertia. **Inertia** is the tendency of any object to remain at rest unless force is applied to it. Because the pen is attached by a string that can **pivot** (turn) at the top, the force your friends applied to the table isn't transmitted to the pen. The heavier an object is, the more force it takes to overcome the inertia of an object. That's why you attached the washers to the pen: to make it harder to put the weighted pen in motion.

Answers from the Past

A Chinese scholar named Chang Heng invented a seismoscope, a device for detecting earthquakes, in A.D. 132. It was shaped like a jar with eight small dragon heads poking out of its upper edge. A ball was balanced in the mouth of each dragon. At the base of the jar under each dragon, there was a frog looking up with a wide-open mouth. When an earthquake occurred, it shook the jar and caused the balls to drop into the frog's mouth, making a noise.

(Courtesy of Laurel Aiello.)

Seismoscope is made of two Greek words: *seismo*, meaning "a quake," and scope, which means "a device for viewing." A seismoscope is a device that allows you to "see" an earthquake. *Graph* in Greek means drawn or written, so a **seismograph** draws or records a quake.

More than 1,800 years later, in 1703, a Frenchman named Jean de la Haute Feuille proposed another seismoscope. He filled a bowl to the brim with mercury, so when an earthquake struck, the mercury would spill over the brim. The mercury would spill away from the source of the earthquake. By noting the direction of the spill and measuring how much mercury spilled, de la Haute Feuille hoped to determine the **epicenter** (the starting point) of the earthquake and its relative size. Because he knew that large quakes were often preceded by smaller ones, de la Haute Feuille also hoped, by noting small quakes, to warn people that a larger one might be on its way.

On February 4, 1783, a series of earthquakes struck in Calabria, Italy, causing an estimated 50,000 deaths. The quakes also inspired clockmaker Domemico Salsano to build what he called, in Italian, a *geo-sismometro*, or "earthquake-measurer."

The pendulum in Salsano's device was about 8½ feet (2.6 meters) tall. The weight attached to the lower end of the pendulum had a brush attached to it. When the pendulum moved, the brush recorded the motion with ink on an ivory slab.

The first problem to solve in measuring earthquakes is how to keep the measuring device still while the earth is shaking. Salsano's pendulum seismograph solved the problem, and it became widely used. An American, Daniel Drake, wrote of using one to measure earthquakes in Cincinnati in 1812.

Seismology, (the study of the earth's movements) developed along with the devices to measure the earth's movements. By combining the findings of **geology** (the study of the earth) with the data from seismographs, scientists gradually came to a more sophisticated understanding of earthquakes. Despite today's precision seismographs, de la Haute Feuille's hope to predict earthquakes has yet to be realized. Earthquakes still often take us by surprise.

What happens if your friends stand at the other sides of the table and jiggle it back and forth? Try it. The seismograph doesn't record much, does it? That's because movement can only be recorded when it is **perpendicular** (crossing at a right angle) to the motion of the tape. As a practical matter, this means it takes two seismographs to measure the horizontal motion of the earth.

The earth can also move vertically. The earth's crust is made up of huge **tectonic plates** (sections of the earth's crust) that move slowly (about 6 inches [15 cm] per year) on the mantle of the earth beneath. Sometimes, when two plates collide with one another, one plate slides under or over the other. When that happens, the resulting earthquake causes vertical motion. A third seismograph is needed to measure vertical motion. Today, scientists use at least three seismographs to record all aspects of earthquake motion.

Seismologists (scientists who study movements in the earth) use the Richter scale to compare earthquakes. The scale starts at 1 and goes to 10. You don't feel earthquakes that measure 2 or below. Moderate earthquakes measure about 6 on the Richter scale.

The scale is a logarithmic scale, which means each number is 10 times greater than the number preceding it. You might think that an earthquake that measures 7 on the Richter scale is just a bit bigger than one that measures 6. In fact, it is 10 times more powerful than an earthquake that measures 6. The quake that killed as many as 750,000 people in Tangshan, China, in 1976 measured 8 on the Richter scale.

INVENTOR'S CHALLENGE

Can you make a seismograph that measures vertical movement?

CLUE

A spring could be useful.

21 Portable Solar Distiller

The Problem

It is 1942 and World War II, the war between Nazi Germany, Italy, and Japan on one side and the United States, Great Britain, France, and other allies on the other side, is raging. You are Dr. Maria Telkes, an American engineer already well known for your research in **solar** (the sun's) energy. The U.S. government has asked for your assistance in the war effort.

The U.S. Navy has hundreds of ships of all sizes engaged in ocean battles against the Japanese Navy. When a ship has been attacked and is sinking, sailors climb into small, open life rafts, and wait for rescue. The U.S. Navy is concerned that the survivors might have to wait a long time before they are found.

People can only live a few days without fresh water to drink. The government has asked you to develop a device that uses the sun's energy to turn salty ocean water into fresh drinking water. Because the device will be used on life rafts, it must be lightweight and unbreakable. Space is limited in a life raft, so the solar still, or distiller, has to float outside the life raft.

Observations

As a solar energy expert, you have studied traditional solar stills, but they are made of metal and glass. They are large, heavy, and the glass is breakable. Clear plastics have recently become available, but will they work?

MATERIALS

clean, empty plastic cup with a clear, domed cover (slushy drinks are served in such containers)

scissors

scotch tape

small, dark-colored plastic cup

glass or cup

¼ cup (50 ml) warm water

spoon

¼ teaspoon (1 ml) salt

Experiment

1. Take the domed cover off the cup. Cut a piece of scotch tape just large enough to cover the hole in the domed cover. Press the tape over the hole.

2. Cut around the small, dark-colored cup about 1 inch (2.5 cm) from the bottom of the cup. You will have a small cup with sides about 1 inch (2.5 cm) high.

3. Cut two pieces of scotch tape that are about twice as long as the diameter of the large cup.

4. Put one piece of tape, sticky side up, on a table. Put the other piece perpendicular (at a 90° angle) to the first so that the pieces of tape form a cross. Center the bottom of the small cup over the intersections of the pieces of tape and press down so that the cup sticks to the tape.

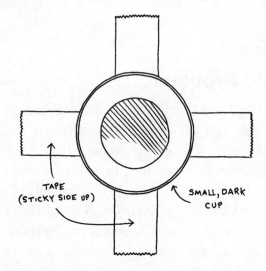

TAPE (STICKY SIDE UP)

SMALL, DARK CUP

5. Cut four pieces of tape about 2 inches (5 cm) long and have them ready to use.

6. Drape the ends of the tape attached to the small cup over the top of the large cup so that the small cup is suspended just below the rim of the large cup. Make sure the small cup is level. Use the four short pieces of tape to secure the ends of the four long pieces of tape to the outside of the large cup.

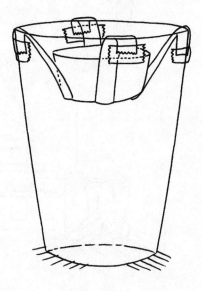

7. Pour the warm water into a glass or cup. Stir in the salt. Taste a little bit of the water: this is your salty ocean water!

8. Find a flat surface where direct sunlight will shine on your experiment for several hours. A sunny outdoor spot in the summer is ideal, but an indoor windowsill that gets direct sunlight can also work. You can also position a desk lamp so that its bulb is several inches from the dome.

9. Place the large cup on the flat surface. Carefully spoon salt water into the small cup until the water is about 1/4 inch (.5 cm) deep in the cup. Make sure no salt water gets into the large cup.

10. Carefully place the domed cover on the large cup.

11. Leave your experiment undisturbed for several hours. After a while, you will see water droplets on the inside of the dome. Eventually, the droplets will slide down the dome into the bottom of the large cup. (You can tap the dome lightly to get the droplets to run down.) When there are at least several drops of water in the large cup, you can stop your experiment, remove (carefully!) the small cup, and taste the water in the large cup. You've made fresh drinking water from salty ocean water!

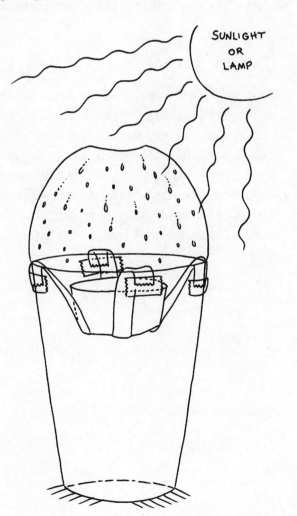

SUNLIGHT OR LAMP

When the sunlight passes through the clear dome, it strikes and heats the water in the cup. The hot water on the surface of the cup **vaporizes**, which means it changes from a liquid to a gas. The vapor is lighter than air, and it rises. When the vapor touches the dome, it cools (because the dome is cooler than the vapor) and **condenses** (changes back to a liquid) as water droplets. Eventually, the water droplets slide down to the bottom of the cup.

The water is not salty because the salt does not rise with the water vapor. Salt is too heavy. If you let your experiment run long enough, there would be nothing but salt left in the little cup.

Answers from the Past

The process you used to turn salty water into fresh water is called **distillation.** Distillation purifies a substance by vaporizing a liquid and then condensing it. Your invention used the concentrated heat of the sun or a lamp to purify salt water. Your invention and others like it are called solar distillers or **solar stills.**

In France in the 1860s, Augustin Mouchot, a professor of mathematics at the Lycée de Pours, invented a number of solar devices, including a solar still. His device used a large metal pan covered by a tight-fitting, tilted pane of glass. A thin layer of the water to be purified covered the pan. The vapor condensed on the inner surface of the glass, ran down the tilted pane of glass, and collected in a channel around the lower edge of the device. The largest solar still of this kind was built in Chile in 1872. It covered an area roughly the size of a football field and produced 6,000 gallons of fresh water per day!

Dr. Maria Telkes was born in Budapest, Hungary, in 1900. She went to high school, college, and graduate school in Hungary and earned a doctorate in physical chemistry at the University of Budapest. In 1925, she emigrated to the United States and started her lifelong career studying energy. First, she studied the energy produced by the body's cells and then began work in the new field of solar energy engineering. One of her first inventions was a house heated by the reaction between sunlight and a common chemical called Glauber's salt.

Soon after the United States entered World War II, Telkes was asked to design a solar still that could be used on life rafts. Stationary (nonmovable) solar stills had been around for almost 80 years, but a solar still for a life raft had to be portable and compact and had to float outside the raft.

Telkes took advantage of the new plastics that were being developed at the time. Her solar still was a round, inflatable envelope of plastic. Inflated, it looked like a slightly flattened, spherical balloon, black on the bottom and clear on the top. In the middle of the balloon, suspended like your cup, was a thin, black absorbent pad on a plastic tray. A tube extended from the tray into the ocean so that the thin pad was always filled with ocean water. The distilled water trickled down the clear roof of the balloon and collected in a chamber at the bottom. Her still produced several pints of water per day.

Telkes's solar stills were put in many U.S. Navy life rafts. They were standard equipment in these rafts through the 1950s. Today, the U.S. Navy supplies its life rafts with distillers that use battery power to force water through a membrane to strain out the salt. However, you can find solar stills much like the one Telkes invented in some marine supply stores. Some recreational boaters carry solar stills for use in an emergency.

INVENTOR'S CHALLENGE

Your solar still can't produce very much fresh water because only a small surface area of salty water is exposed to the sun's rays. Design and make a solar still that will produce more water. Consider Telkes's and Mouchot's designs. Have a competition with some friends: Who can make a still that produces the greatest amount of fresh water?

[22] Mousetrap

The Problem

You've got a mouse in your house, and it's got to go. You've looked at all the mousetraps on the market, and you're sure you can build a better one.

You make a trip to the U.S. Patent Office to get advice from a patent officer. She tells you the Patent Office has already awarded over 4,400 patents for mousetraps since 1838, and your mousetrap has to be substantially different from the other 4,400 to win a patent. The Patent Office, she adds, doesn't care whether an invention is practical or efficient, as long as it works and is unlike any already patented invention. As you prepare to leave, the patent officer whispers two words to you—*Rube Goldberg*—and winks.

Observations

You look up Rube Goldberg and learn that he was an American cartoonist who was most popular from about 1910 to 1935. When Goldberg started cartooning at the beginning of the twentieth century, inventors seemed to be producing something new every day. Cars, telephones, simple cameras, radios, and revolving doors were just a few of the inventions that became popular in the first three decades of the 1900s.

Goldberg was intrigued by the fantastic new inventions and bought many of them. However, he and many other people found that the inventions didn't always work as promised and were often frustrating. The wonderful gadgets also had some not-so-wonderful consequences. For example, radios and telephones meant less peace and quiet. Cars made life hazardous for pedestrians. Cameras invaded privacy.

Goldberg captured Americans' mixed feelings about these modern contraptions in his famous *Inventions of Professor Butts* cartoons, which he drew from 1909 to 1935. In each cartoon, the professor demonstrates a machine that accomplishes a simple task, such as closing a window, but does so in such an absurdly complex and inefficient way that you have to laugh.

After taking a look at Professor Butts's inventions, you know what to do. You're going to make a Rube Goldberg mousetrap.

> **G**oldberg's cartoons were so popular that **Rube Goldberg** became an adjective defined in the dictionary. It means "having a fantastically complicated, improvised appearance."

MATERIALS

Choose some (or all!) of the materials from the following list. You can add other items, but no saws, hammers, knives, or other materials that require adult help. Your mouse can be a small ball or toy car (if you want the mouse to run into the trap), or you can make a mouse out of modeling clay (if the trap comes to the mouse). Use a large sheet of corrugated cardboard or a piece of plywood as a sturdy base.

paper, cardboard, corrugated cardboard, poster board, acetate sheets

pencils, pens, rulers, scissors, wire cutters

modeling clay

paper clips, paper brads, glue, string, tape, packing tape, thumbtacks

Mouse Eliminator

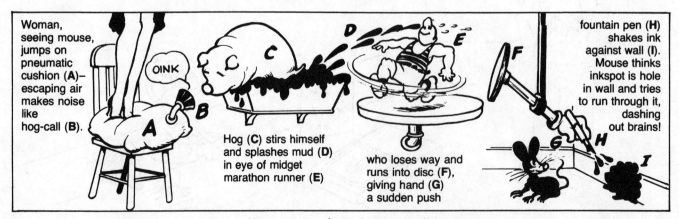

Woman, seeing mouse, jumps on pneumatic cushion (**A**)—escaping air makes noise like hog-call (**B**).

OINK

Hog (**C**) stirs himself and splashes mud (**D**) in eye of midget marathon runner (**E**)

who loses way and runs into disc (**F**), giving hand (**G**) a sudden push

fountain pen (**H**) shakes ink against wall (**I**). Mouse thinks inkspot is hole in wall and tries to run through it, dashing out brains!

Reprinted by permission of United Feature Syndicate, Inc.

paper, plastic, or Styrofoam cups, plates, bowls

cereal, shoe, or tissue boxes, potato chip cans, plastic bottles

Ping-Pong balls or other small balls

small stones, marbles, beads, empty spools of thread

Popsicle sticks, tongue depressors, coffee stirrers, straws

D cell batteries, magnets, bell wire, wire strippers, alligator clips

toy cars, balloons, bells, kitchen funnels, bamboo skewers, springs

Legos and other kinds of building blocks

water

Experiment

1. Draw a design for a mousetrap that involves at least four steps.

2. Gather your supplies.

3. Start at the last step (the device that catches the mouse) and work backward to the first step.

Answers from the Past

Rats and mice have been a problem for humankind since ancient times. A single mouse can eat up to 4 pounds (1.8 kg) of grain a year. Since a pair of mice can produce 100,000 descendants in one year, you can see what a huge problem mice can be.

Rodents, including mice, also carry bacteria and viruses that cause diseases. During the Middle Ages, rats became a deadly danger because they carried bubonic plague. Fleas bit infected rats, and when the fleas then bit people, the people caught the plague.

The earliest description we have of a rat or mousetrap (other than a cat) is from Europe in A.D. 1170. The trap

that was described had "a blade poised above, ready to fall, strike, and pin, and triggered to be released and fall at the slightest touch." In early America, blacksmiths and other craftsmen built their own unpatented devices. Some were designed so that mice fell through hinged doors and into a container of water. Some tipped a heavy object onto the mouse when the mouse touched the trigger. Many involved knives. All were rather gruesome.

The first commercial mousetrap in the United States was designed, patented, and pro-

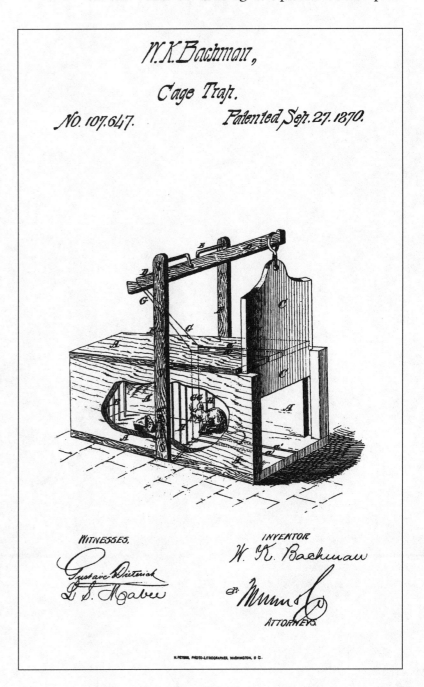

duced in 1838. In the following decades, hundreds more designs were patented. Most of the devices killed their victims, but the Patent Office also issued several patents that trapped mice alive. One popular device invented in 1876 advertised that it captured 5 to 15 live mice in a box-like container. That basic design became the Haveaheart live traps used today.

The familiar snap trap was invented in 1899. It was cheap, effective, and killed the mouse quickly by breaking its spine without much mess. The snap trap was a near-perfect solution to trapping mice, but that didn't stop inventors. The Patent Office issued thousands of patents in the twentieth century, including those for devices that blow up mice with gunpowder, electrocute them, hit them with laser beams, chase them away with low sound frequencies, and trap them in glue.

There are still lots of inventors who believe they can build a better mousetrap. Every year, the U.S. Patent Office issues patents for mousetraps. Maybe yours will be one!

Glossary

airfoil: an object with a curved surface that produces lift by creating less air pressure on the object's upper surface than on its lower surface.

aqueduct: trough or pipe that transports water, which in ancient Rome often rested on top of arches.

arch: a curved structure that extends across an opening or serves as a support.

arch dam: a dam that controls the flow of river water by distributing the weight of the water to riverside cliffs or banks by means of a curved barrier.

backwash: the turbulent air that flows off the end of an object as it moves through air or water.

bellows: an accordion-shaped device with a nozzle that creates and directs a stream of air.

biconvex: having two outwardly curving surfaces.

bottle organ: a musical instrument that produces notes when air is pushed over and into the mouths of glass bottles.

bow: the front of a boat.

camera lucida: a nineteenth-century lens and mirror system that artists used to project an image on paper.

chemical energy: energy that bonds atoms together.

clepsydra: the ancient Greek name for a water clock, a device that tells time by the gradual escape of water from a container.

code: a secret message system in which whole words (rather than individual letters as in a cipher) are replaced.

coffer dams: hollow, cylindrical structures that are built in the water to create a dry space where a bridge pier can be constructed.

combustion chamber: a place in a rocket where chemical fuels are mixed to produce the hot gases that propel the rocket.

compression: the force that tends to squeeze matter together.

condense: cool a vapor so that it changes into a liquid.

conduct: pass by direct contact.

conning tower: the low, broad tower on top of a submarine used for observation and entry.

convex: outwardly curving.

cryptographer: a person who makes codes and ciphers.

decibel: a unit of measurement of the loudness of sounds.

distillation: the purification of a liquid by vaporizing and condensing it.

drag: the friction created by contact of a moving object with a gas, liquid, or solid.

epicenter: the point from which the shock waves of an earthquake radiate.

fired: baked at high temperature in a kiln until hard.

fissure: a long, narrow opening.

frequency: the rate of recurrence.

friction: a force that slows down a moving object that is in contact with a gas, liquid, or solid.

geology: the study of the earth.

gimbal: a device consisting of a frame of rings moving freely on pivots used to keep an object, such as a compass, in a horizontal position.

gravity dam: a dam in which the sheer weight of material piled up in the path of a river prevents the water from following its natural course.

gyroscope: a gimbal that has a spinning wheel as the object in its center. Once the gyroscope's wheel has been set in motion, it stays pointed in the same direction and at the same angle to Earth no matter how the frame of rings around it is moved.

heat energy: a form of energy that is made evident in heat.

hovercraft: a vehicle that is suspended and propelled above land or water by moving air.

hull: the hollow, lowermost portion of a boat that excludes water from the vessel's interior.

inertia: the tendency of any object to remain at rest until force is applied to it.

insulate: to reduce the transfer of heat from an object to an adjacent solid, liquid, or gas.

kaleidoscope: a tube that contains small objects or pieces of glass at one end and at the other end has a cap with a hole for viewing those objects against incoming light.

kazoo: a modern version of a mirliton, a primitive instrument that consists of a hollow tube or sphere with three holes: one to blow into, one for breath to exit, and one that is covered by a membrane whose vibration produces sound waves.

kinetoscope: a nineteenth-century, hand-cranked precursor of the movie projector.

lift: an upward force that is created by the difference in air pressure above and below a curved surface as the curved object moves through air or water.

magnify: enlarge.

mechanical energy: a form of energy that is manifested in motion.

mirliton: a primitive instrument that consists of a hollow tube or sphere with three holes: one to blow into, one for breath to exit, and one that is covered by a membrane whose vibration produces sound waves.

obelisk: a tall, tapering pillar with four sides.

parachute: a folding device shaped like an umbrella that is used to slow the fall of a person or object from the sky.

pendulum: a rod with a weight at the end suspended so that it swings back and forth by the action of gravity.

periscope: a tube with a series of mirrors inside that allows a viewer to see objects that would otherwise be blocked from view. Periscopes are often used in submarines to see above the surface of water.

permafrost: land that is frozen year-round.

perpendicular: crossing at or forming a right angle.

persistence of vision: the phenomenon whereby a visual image is briefly retained by the brain after the image is no longer there.

phenakistiscope: a toy that exploits the persistence of vision phenomenon and consists of a spinning disk with pictures in a sequence on its surface.

photon: a particle of light energy.

pier: a support that raises the road surface of a bridge above water or land.

pitch: (1) a gooey, black substance used to seal the joints in boats' hulls; (2) the highness or lowness of sounds.

pivot: turn.

polarize: to make light travel in one plane.

presbyopia: an inability to see close objects clearly.

radiate: emit energy in the form of rays or waves (not by direct contact).

reflect: to bounce back light.

refract: to bend light.

reservoir: a place where a large amount of water has been collected and stored for use.

resonator: in a musical instrument, the space filled with air that amplifies sound, such as the body of a guitar or a kazoo.

Rube Goldberg: having a fantastically complicated, improvised appearance.

scytale: a method of secret writing in ancient Greece in which a message was written on a strip of parchment that wound in a spiral around a wooden cylinder or cone. The message became incomprehensible when the parchment was unrolled, and could be read only when rewound on an identical piece of wood.

seismograph: a device that makes a visual record and measures the intensity of an earthquake.

seismologists: scientists who study earthquakes.

seismology: the science and study of earthquakes.

seismoscope: a device for detecting an earthquake shock, which sometimes also indicates (without measuring) its intensity or direction.

sodium carbonate: a chemical found in the ashes of burned vegetation or as deposits in the earth.

solar still: a device that purifies water by vaporizing and condensing it.

solar: related to the sun.

sound waves: vibrations moving through air or water that the ear can sense.

stern: the rear of a boat.

stethoscope: a device that gathers sound waves and directs them to the ear or ears, frequently used to listen to the heartbeat.

substitution cipher: a secret message system in which every letter is substituted with another letter.

suspension bridge: a bridge that is held in place by ropes or cables under tension.

tectonic plates: large sections of the earth's crust that move and whose collision causes earthquakes.

tension: a pulling force that tends to stretch a material.

thaumatrope: a two-sided, spinning disk toy that exploits the persistence of vision phenomenon.

thermodynamics: the science of the relationship between heat, energy, and work.

transposition cipher: a secret message system in which the sender rearranges the letters of a message and the receiver has a key to put them back in order.

tune: to adjust the sounds that a musical instrument produces.

unglazed pot: a fired clay pot that does not have a shiny surface.

vacuum: a space that is empty of all matter.

vaporize: to change from a liquid to a gas.

vibrate: to move back and forth rapidly.

water clock: a device that tells time by the gradual escape of water from a container.

water pressure: the force created by the weight of water.

water vapor: water that fills space like a gas, such as steam.

zoetrope: a toy that exploits the persistence of vision phenomenon and consists of a rotating drum with pictures in a sequence on its interior surface.

Index